STANLEY BARRACKS

STANLEY BARRACKS

Toronto's Military Legacy

ALDONA SENDZIKAS
FOREWORD BY DESMOND MORTON

NATURAL HERITAGE BOOKS
A MEMBER OF THE DUNDURN GROUP
TORONTO

Copyright ©Aldona Sendzikas, 2011

All rights reserved. No part of this publication may be reproduced, stored in a retrieval system, or transmitted in any form or by any means, electronic, mechanical, photocopying, recording, or otherwise (except for brief passages for purposes of review) without the prior permission of Dundurn Press. Permission to photocopy should be requested from Access Copyright.

Editor: Jane Gibson
Copy-Editor: Shannon Whibbs
Design: Jennifer Scott
Printer: Marquis

Library and Archives Canada Cataloguing in Publication

Sendzikas, Aldona
    Stanley Barracks : Toronto's military legacy / by Aldona Sendzikas.

Includes bibliographical references and index.
Issued also in electronic format.
ISBN 978-1-55488-788-0

1. Stanley Barracks (Toronto, Ont.)--History. 2. Toronto (Ont.)--History, Military. 3. Canada. Canadian Army--Barracks and quarters--History--19th century. 4. Canada. Canadian Army--Barracks and quarters--History--20th century. 5. Great Britain. Army--Barracks and quarters--History--19th century. 6. Civil-military relations--Ontario--Toronto--History. 7. Historic sites--Ontario--Toronto. I. Title.

FC3097.8.S73S46 2011   971.3'541   C2010-902702-7

1 2 3 4 5   15 14 13 12 11

We acknowledge the support of the **Canada Council for the Arts** and the **Ontario Arts Council** for our publishing program. We also acknowledge the financial support of the **Government of Canada** through the **Canada Book Fund**, and **Livres Canada Books**, and the **Government of Ontario** through the **Ontario Book Publishers Tax Credit** program, and the **Ontario Media Development Corporation**.

Care has been taken to trace the ownership of copyright material used in this book. The author and the publisher welcome any information enabling them to rectify any references or credits in subsequent editions.
                                                                    J. Kirk Howard, President

Printed and bound in Canada.
www.dundurn.com

Published by Natural Heritage Books
A Member of The Dundurn Group

Dundurn Press	Gazelle Book Services Limited	Dundurn Press
3 Church Street, Suite 500	White Cross Mills	2250 Military Road
Toronto, Ontario, Canada	High Town, Lancaster, England	Tonawanda, NY
M5E 1M2	LA1 4XS	U.S.A. 14150

CONTENTS

Foreword by Desmond Morton	7
Preface	9
Acknowledgements	13
Chapter One: The British Period (1840–1870)	**15**
The "Old Fort"	15
The "New Fort"	18
A British Garrison: Life in the New Fort	25
The Withdrawal of British Forces from Canada	44
Chapter Two: The Canadian Period (1870–1914)	**47**
The Dominion Government Takes Over the New Fort	47
The North-West Mounted Police	52
The Infantry School	65
The Permanent Force	82
Chapter Three: The World Wars (1914–1945)	**93**
"Exhibition Camp"	93
The Internment of "Enemy Aliens"	106
Between the Wars	114
"C.N.E. Camp"	129

Chapter Four: The Post-War Years (1945 to Today)	141
Emergency Housing	141
Demolition	147
The Last Building Standing	154
Notes	159
Bibliography	185
Index	205
About the Author	213

FOREWORD

School for War: Stanley Barracks and Toronto's Exhibition Grounds

Toronto was once a very military town. Its high-school students, male and female, were drilled and paraded for an annual inspection under the beaming approval of Toronto's inspector of schools, James L. Hughes. Its two oldest militia regiments, the 2nd Queen's Own Rifles and the 10th Royal Grenadiers, paraded proudly on ceremonial and celebratory occasions, as befitted two of the most respected and efficient units in Canada. When it was Toronto's turn to boast of its own kilted regiment, the 48th Highlanders sprang to life at full strength and fully accouterd within weeks of authorization. Working people and the wealthy worked together to give the city the best military institutions they could muster as proof of their commitment to the British imperialism that held sway in Canada's Queen City.

Military zeal may have been a little easier in Toronto because, hidden away in the city's vast Exhibition grounds, was Stanley Barracks, home to some of the strongest units of Canada's tiny professional army. At the Barracks, militia volunteers could see for themselves how professional soldiers in "C" Company of the Infantry School Corps (now the Royal Canadian Regiment) drilled, handled their weapons, and submitted to the uncompromising discipline which, to this day, distinguishes real soldiers from the overconfident amateurs. Those who aspired to Toronto's Governor General's Body Guard could model themselves on the trim, spotlessly turned-out troopers of the Cavalry School Corps, now the

Royal Canadian Dragoons. The unofficial motto of the Royal Canadian Regiment was and is, "Never pass a fault." It was born on this parade square.

Other would-be Canadian soldiers had to judge their appearance in their own mirrors or from the admiring comments of friends or family; Toronto militiamen, afflicted with forgetfulness or a fancy for unauthorized ornament, ran the risk of a harsh and humiliating bark from a sergeant from "The Barracks." Remember that a soldier on constant alert is more likely to survive a hostile battlefield and to contribute to any victory.

The surviving remnant of Stanley Barracks, described by Dr. Sendzikas, was only the centrepiece of a vast arena that created soldiers for Canada in the First World War and airmen, primarily, for the Second. The barns and halls of the Canadian National Exhibition grounds became makeshift barracks in both world wars and the training schools for men and women who formed the core of Toronto's contribution to the Allied cause. Stanley Barracks and the older Exhibition buildings that hide it survive today as functioning memorials to those Torontonians who offered their lives to their country after 1914 and again in 1939, and who often paid with their lives for Allied victory.

Times have changed. It now takes more than a drill square and a rifle range to train an effective soldier. It now requires open terrain and an even tougher physical regimen to prepare for war in an electronic age. Cities too have changed, and the limited space they could allot for soldiering within their own perimeter is needed now for a city's own business. Stanley Barracks and its neighbours remind us of the men and women who met there, sacrificing creature comforts to prepare themselves for their country's battles. A former student, Aldona Sendzikas has worked hard to help us all understand our city and its heritage a little better. I share and celebrate the results of her labour.

Desmond Morton, C.D., O.C., F.R.S.C.
Professor of History Emeritus
University of Toronto

PREFACE

In the years 1840 and 1841, on the shore of Lake Ontario and on a plot of land that is now part of downtown Toronto, the Royal Engineers of the British Army constructed a massive stone fort consisting of six main buildings around a parade square. Designed to house three hundred men, this new fort was built to replace Toronto's original military garrison, Fort York, located approximately one kilometre to the east. Fort York, situated strategically at the mouth of Toronto Harbour, had served since 1793 as Toronto's primary defence, but by the 1830s was falling into disrepair.

The decision to construct a new British fortification in Toronto in 1840 to replace the "Old Fort" made it clear that, despite the expense of building and manning colonial garrisons, the British government saw a need to keep up a strong military presence in its Canadian colonies. Events such as the rebellions in Upper and Lower Canada in 1837–38, and the seizure and destruction of the American steamer *Caroline* by Canadian militiamen in what became known as the "*Caroline* affair" in 1838, had led to deteriorating Anglo-American relations and signalled to the British government that if it intended to hold on to the colonies that British troops had defended successfully from American annexation in the War of 1812, then Britain had to maintain its garrisons in the colonies, despite the cost.

The "New Fort," as it became known, would become the main British Army facility in Toronto. As such, it would exert a considerable amount of influence on the city. Early Toronto can be classified as a "garrison town," not only because it began through the establishment of a garrison, but because the continued existence of the garrison played a key role in setting the tone of local society. The presence of a British garrison shaped Canadian military development by serving as a model, and setting standards of efficiency, for the Canadian militia and Permanent Force. In many ways, the garrison also affected the lives of the citizens of Toronto. The very visible presence of a large force of red-coated soldiers helped to cement Canada's connection with Britain, while encouraging Canadians to resist American influences, and to make Toronto a centre of martial spirit. Troops from the garrison were actively involved in the life of the city: they were often called in to assist civilian authorities in dealing with disturbances in town, or to serve as firefighters when one of Toronto's buildings caught ablaze. The officers of the garrison, clad in the distinctive scarlet tunic of the British Army, enjoyed an active social life, since they were very popular additions to social functions in the city and received numerous invitations to parties and dances. But they had to be wary: more than a few parents with daughters of marrying age eyed these British officers as perfect potential sons-in-law. For decades, in addition to its military role, the New Fort would serve as an important social centre for the city of Toronto.

Even after the withdrawal of British troops from Canada in 1870, the New Fort (renamed Stanley Barracks in 1893) would continue to play a key role in the life of Toronto, as well as in the history of the country as a whole. Few historic sites can boast of such a colourful and varied history. In 1874, the newly formed North-West Mounted Police — a paramilitary force created to patrol and maintain order in the newly acquired Northwest Territory, and the brainchild of Prime Minister Sir John A. Macdonald — trained some of its first recruits at the New Fort. In 1883, when Canadian infantry and cavalry schools were established to train the Canadian militia, part of this new Canadian Permanent Force was located in the New Fort, giving Toronto its garrison once again, this time, a Canadian one, although based on the British model. These schools would develop into a company of the Royal Canadian Regiment and the Royal Canadian Dragoons.

Preface

Over the succeeding years, the Toronto garrison grew at times of major military conflicts, as Stanley Barracks served as a concentration centre for troops before their dispatch to battle zones. During the First World War, numerous units of the Canadian Expeditionary Force were assembled and trained at the New Fort and the surrounding Canadian National Exhibition grounds and buildings before being sent overseas. During the Second World War, Stanley Barracks and Exhibition Park again were transformed into recruitment and training centres for the Canadian military. There is a darker side, as well. During the First World War, Stanley Barracks served as a prison for those whom the Canadian government labelled as "enemy-aliens."

But Toronto kept expanding; the Canadian National Exhibition was growing in success and attendance figures, and the C.N.E. Association needed more land. Throughout its history, Stanley Barracks was engaged in its own private battle, one of survival in the face of the expansion of the "Ex." As the C.N.E. continued to expand, various buildings of Stanley Barracks were turned over by the Dominion government to the City. With the end of the Second World War, the military was instructed to vacate the buildings of Stanley Barracks. However, since Toronto found itself facing a severe postwar housing shortage, City and C.N.E. officials put their plans for the New Fort on hold, while the City used Stanley Barracks as emergency civilian housing. When the last civilian tenants moved out in 1951, Toronto proceeded with the demolition of the Stanley Barracks buildings. Outraged preservationists protested what seemed to them the wilful destruction of history. Municipal "progress," however, had the upper hand. By 1953, all of the buildings of Stanley Barracks except one — the officers' quarters — had been demolished.

The officers' quarters still stands today, separated from Lake Ontario by the busy Lake Shore Boulevard thoroughfare, and surrounded on its three other sides by row upon row of parking spaces. These days, when someone speaks of "Stanley Barracks," they more likely than not are referring to this one building, unaware that Stanley Barracks, not so long ago, was in fact a formidable collection of six such massive stone buildings, surrounded by numerous auxiliary structures and a defensive picket enclosure. Located within Exhibition Place (as Toronto's Exhibition grounds are now known), seen by millions of C.N.E. visitors over the years and by millions more people as they drive along Lake Shore Boulevard, the sand-coloured stone structure that is the last surviving remnant of Stanley Barracks is such a familiar feature of the architectural landscape of this part of Toronto, that few probably give it a second thought. Yet this single building holds a million memories; it stands silently but proudly as the last bastion of the preservation of a long and colourful piece of Toronto's history. The story of Stanley Barracks is the story of the last facility manned by the British military in Toronto. It is also the story of the development of Canada's own Permanent Force; of Canadian participation in armed conflict, including two world wars; and of the precarious balance between civil-military relations, as the expansion of Toronto and its annual Exhibition encroached upon the lands and buildings of Stanley Barracks. It is also the story about the battle of historic preservation — a battle that Stanley Barracks, and its modern-day defenders, lost.

Yet, amidst the concrete lots and parked cars, the one remaining building of Toronto's New Fort holds it ground, protected from the possibility of demolition by its official designation in 1998 as a heritage site, in turn protecting Toronto's military legacy.

ACKNOWLEDGEMENTS

My interest in Stanley Barracks began when I was employed at Historic Fort York in the late 1980s, at which time the fort was operated and managed by the Toronto Historical Board. The Board's administrative offices were located in the Stanley Barracks officers' quarters, along with the Marine Museum of Upper Canada, which the Board also managed. Visits to this building in the normal course of the day piqued my interest in the New Fort, and in its remarkable, but as of yet unrecorded, history. My research was encouraged and supported by the Board, in particular by Dr. Carl Benn, former curator of Historic Fort York and author of *Historic Fort York, 1793–1993*.

Numerous other individuals, many of them former Fort York staff, assisted me in various ways throughout this project, and I would like to take this opportunity to thank them. Jamie Maxwell and Scott Woodland put themselves on call for proofreading duties and offered helpful comments and advice. Jamie also took photographs of the Stanley Barracks officers' quarters that appear in this book. John Summers and Wendy Cooper, who used to have their offices in the officers' quarters, shared their memories of the building with me. Chris Laverton generously shared his own research with me, and also alerted me to the existence of the previously unpublished 1848 image of the New Fort, recently discovered in the collection of Alan Mortimer. Thanks are also due to Mr. Mortimer, who provided me with a copy of this image, along with one of

Fort York, and kindly allowed me to include them in this book. I am also grateful to Ron Ridley, curator of Fort Henry in Kingston, who put me in touch with Mr. Mortimer. Richard Haynes and the present-day staff of Historic Fort York allowed me free access to the Fort York archives, which includes some Stanley Barracks-related material.

Linda Cobon, manager of records and archives at Exhibition Place, Toronto, has been the frequent source of quick and cheerful assistance, both in accessing relevant information in the archives of the C.N.E., and in tracking down sources and photographs. Karen Hansen of Hansen Designs in London, Ontario, once again demonstrated great talent and patience in creating the map on page 68. I am also indebted to Timo Puhakka for providing photos of the former gates of Stanley Barracks, now located at Guildwood Village.

I have been fortunate in having the services of an enthusiastic research assistant, Zale Skolnik, one of my former students, who cheerfully and conscientiously undertook a variety of tasks, from tracking down photographs to fact-checking. Another student, Laura McGee, assisted in newspaper research. My thanks to all the others who offered advice or assistance in one form or another along the way; all of it was helpful and I am grateful to these individuals. They include include Dr. Jonathan Vance, Claus Breede, Dr. Rob Vaughan, Paul Cheshire, Melanie Garrison, and Ramute Palys. My thanks, as well, to the individuals who, over the years, have shared their personal knowledge and recollections of life in the New Fort.

Finally, I owe thanks to Dr. Desmond Morton, my former professor of Canadian military history at the University of Toronto. I am honoured to have my former teacher and one of Canada's greatest military historians — as well as the grandson of one of Stanley Barracks' most eminent residents, Sir William Dillon Otter — write the foreword for this book.

CHAPTER ONE

The British Period (1840–1870)

THE "OLD FORT"

It is not surprising that Toronto would become the site of a major British military garrison. The significance of the area was recognized as early as 1788 by British authorities, and by French fur traders and Canadian Natives well before that. Toronto was part of an important Native trail linking Lake Ontario with Lake Huron, a trail that became important for European settlers because of the fur trade. Among the forts built by the French in North America to strengthen their fur supply route was Fort Rouillé (also known as Fort Toronto), located at the foot of present-day Dufferin Street. During the Seven Years' War (1756–1763), Fort Rouille was destroyed and the site abandoned by the French themselves in order to prevent its occupation by the British.

In 1788, Britain purchased the Toronto site from the Mississauga Natives. Lord Dorchester (Sir Guy Carleton), governor-in-chief of British North America, sent surveyor Alexander Aitkin to the area to lay out a town and garrison site. Dorchester, however, harboured some doubts about the effectiveness of Toronto as a military stronghold, and no further action was taken until 1793. Deteriorating Anglo-American relations prompted Upper Canada's lieutenant governor, Colonel John Graves Simcoe, to establish a naval base at Toronto. Simcoe believed that Toronto was an ideal location, being a safe distance from the American border, and possessing a defensible, sheltered harbour. In July of 1793, one hundred men of the Queen's Rangers, commanded by Simcoe, arrived at Toronto and established a military camp by the shore of Lake Ontario, at the harbour entrance.[1] This camp marked the beginnings of the city of Toronto.

Simcoe named the site "York" in commemoration of a recent battle victory by the Duke of York. He set aside approximately four hundred hectares (one thousand acres) of the site as a military reserve: the area roughly between the lakeshore, and modern day Queen, Peter, and Dufferin Streets.[2] Simcoe's town layout differed somewhat from Aitkin's 1788 survey. In Simcoe's plan, the fort was placed farther east. He explained his choice of location in a letter to the Duke of Richmond: "It is an exceedingly healthy spot, capable of being easily fortified & in that case of essentially contributing to the protection of the Harbour."[3] Settlement in the area grew, especially with the transfer of the provincial capital from Newark (now Niagara-on-the-Lake) to York, a move which was completed by 1798. The garrison served not only as the town's military protector, but as the primary consumer of the town's goods and services. By the end of the eighteenth century, however, most of the original garrison buildings were in poor condition. They were torn down and replaced. In 1811, York's fortifications were further improved, in anticipation of war with the United States.

In June 1812, the United States declared war on Britain. York became a target in the spring of 1813, when American military strategists decided that the capture of British ships at York would help U.S. forces gain control of Lake Ontario. On April 27, an American naval squadron landed west of the fort. In a battle that lasted six hours, the badly outnumbered and outgunned defenders were forced to retreat. A six-day occupation of the town followed. When the American troops finally departed, they left the barracks standing, and the British soon reoccupied York. On July 31, an American squadron returned to York and, this time, burned down the fort barracks. By late August of that year, the British had begun the reconstruction of the fort. Work continued throughout the war, and by 1816, a fort consisting of eighteen buildings had been erected. Seven of these buildings still stand today.

The British Period (1840–1870)

Fort York continued to be garrisoned by the British Army in the years following the War of 1812, the strength of the garrison varying according to the state of international relations. Reinforcements were sent to Canada as a result of the 1837 Rebellion, and by 1838 there were over thirteen thousand British regulars in British North America.[4]

Even before the rebellion crisis, authorities recognized the need to replace Fort York, because it did not offer adequate accommodations or sufficient protection. Its wooden buildings were decaying and infested with vermin; they could hardly be expected to last. In addition, a shifting sandbar made the proposed location for a new fort — one kilometre west of Fort York — now better suited for defence of the harbour.[5]

The availability of funding to build a new and more substantial fortification was a problem, however, and delayed the matter. In 1833, Lieutenant Governor Sir John Colborne came up with a solution. He proposed that the eastern section of the military reserve be sold, and the proceeds used to build the new structures, west of the Old Fort, at a cost of £10,000. Colborne's suggestion would not only provide funds for the project, but would allow the town to expand to the west, where the military reserve was blocking its growth. The British government approved the plan, and later that year lots on the military reserve were laid out and offered up for sale. However, the construction of the fortifications was delayed.[6]

By this time, additional accommodations for the troops at Toronto (as York had been renamed in 1834) were even more desperately needed. As a temporary solution, the military had rented an odd assortment of buildings throughout the city for use as barracks. A barrack inspection report dated August 19, 1840, listed the various buildings in use: they included Osgoode Hall, Mr. Dunn's house and hospital, Mr. Crookshank's, Mr. Chewitt's (or the British Coffee House), Mr. Ritchie's, and Mr. Howell's hospital. The cost to the military for these temporary accommodations amounted to £1,809 per year. The report concluded that: "With regard to these Buildings it is hoped that when the new Barracks … are completed, the necessity will have ceased for so large an Expenditure on account of Rents.…"[7]

The rebellion crisis in the colonies, along with worsening Anglo-American relations, at last inspired some action. In the absence of any serious progress on the construction of a new fort, Sir Francis Bond Head, the lieutenant governor of Upper Canada, authorized the construction of a large barracks building at Fort York. This building would be big enough to house three hundred men. Finally, in June of 1839, the Board of Ordnance authorized the construction of a new fort at Toronto, with barracks accommodation for three hundred, along with the necessary auxiliary buildings. The new fort was based on a revision of a plan submitted by Lieutenant-Colonel Gustavus Nicolls, commander of the Royal Corps of Engineers in Canada, in December 1833. The funds authorized for the construction project totalled £22,853.6.7¼. Of this amount, £10,000 was to be recovered by the provincial government from the sale of military reserve lands. Claims for the additional expenses were to be submitted to Parliament.[8]

THE "NEW FORT"

The new garrison was to be located approximately one kilometre west of the Old Fort — in fact, at the very spot that Aitkin, in his 1788 survey, had proposed as the best location for Toronto's garrison. The actual construction of the New Fort took place between February 1840 and October 1841. The buildings were constructed of stone, brick, or wood. Brick clay and timber were available in the area; however, the only stones found locally were granite boulder stone, unsuitable for building, and another known as "lake stone," which had a laminated nature that caused it to splinter into horizontal fragments when hammered. A more suitable building material was limestone, which could be obtained from Kingston, Queenston, or Hamilton, the latter two places being preferable, since the route between them and Toronto was considerably shorter, and most of the route could be travelled by water. Consequently, the massive stone buildings of the New Fort were built of Queenston limestone, with interior brick partitions, solid stone stairs, and tinned roofs.[9]

The plans for the New Fort called for the construction of an officers' barracks, two privates' barracks, a hospital, an officers' stable, barrack master's stores, an engine house, a gunpowder magazine and a canteen, around a parade square. The estimate for the new fort also included the necessary privies and ash pits, wash house and cleaning sheds, fuel yard, sewers, drains, surface drain, two wells, parade roads, and a barracks enclosure.

The officers' barracks — the one building that still stands today — was to be a large, two-storey structure with thick masonry walls. It was designed to accommodate one field officer, fourteen captains and subalterns, a mess establishment with a wine cellar and larder, servants' quarters, and an office for a barrack master. The building would be located on the south side of the parade square, by the lakeshore. The hospital was to be built on the north side of the square, opposite the officers' quarters. This two-storey building would have room for twenty-four patients, and its facilities would include a surgery stove, a kitchen, a wash house, rooms for a hospital sergeant and nurse, a dead-house (used to temporarily store bodies before burial), privies, and an ash pit. The hospital would also have its own yard, enclosed by a wall.

The larger of the two privates' barracks was designed to accommodate 207 non-commissioned officers and men. It would also include five cells, an orderly room, two guardrooms, and a kitchen. This building was also constructed of masonry, hammered on the face, and featured a "gallery" or veranda, eight feet (2.4 metres) wide, extending along the front of the building on the ground floor. "Range No. 1," as this building was referred to, was located on the east side of the fort. "Range No. 2" privates' barracks, flanking the officers' quarters on the western side of the parade square, opposite the larger range, was to be constructed in the same style, but it was significantly smaller and designed to accommodate only 105 non-commissioned officers and men. It would also house a regimental stove and cooking house.

South of Range No. 2 was the canteen: a two-storey building big enough to serve a garrison of three hundred. The tap room, kitchen, and bar were on the first floor, while the upper level would house a non-commissioned officers' room and two bedrooms. This building also had a basement, which could function as a storage cellar for the canteen.

A building beside the canteen would function as the barrack master's stores, with three barrack storerooms, a small office, and two rooms for the barrack sergeant; it also would accommodate an engine house, a straw store, and a fuel yard. A stable for five horses, with a forage room and dung pit, was planned for east of the officers' quarters, and a magazine, large enough to hold forty barrels of gunpowder, was to be built in the northeast corner of the fort.

The plan also called for privies and ash pits to be provided for each range of officers' and privates' barracks and for the barrack master's stores building, and also for a cleaning shed to be located behind Ranges Nos. 1 and 2, and a wash house behind Range No. 1.[10]

The original plan for the New Fort included surrounding the fort with works of fortification. Colborne's 1833 proposal had recommended that the new "Barracks and Offices" be "enclosed whenever it might be deemed necessary to construct works of defence at this station." However, as part of the overall strategy of trying to reduce, as much as possible, Nicolls's original cost estimate of 1833, the construction of defensive works was postponed. A barrack enclosure of some sort still being necessary, a fence of cedar picketing was proposed, approximately eight feet (2.4 metres) in height, with two gates with wrought iron hinges and "2 strong padlocks." This type of picket fencing was in fact quite common, probably because timber and boards of good quality were readily available in the Toronto area.[11]

The completed fort varied in some additional ways from the original plan. It was decided, for example, that the proposed stabling for five officers' horses was insufficient, as the commanding officer of the New Fort would be permitted two horses, and the barrack master, surgeon, adjutant, and quartermaster would each be allowed one. Therefore, not one, but two stables were in fact built, one on either side of the officers' quarters, each for five horses. In addition, an armourer's shop was deemed necessary, and an 1841 plan of the completed fort shows an armourer's shop in the northeast corner of the barrack enclosure. The magazine, which was supposed to be located in that area, was constructed instead in the northwest corner of the fort.[12]

The main entrance gate to the fort was located on the east side of the compound. It could be reached through an arch in Range No. 1 Barracks, and the road beyond it led directly to the Old Fort, and from there to the

The British Period (1840–1870)

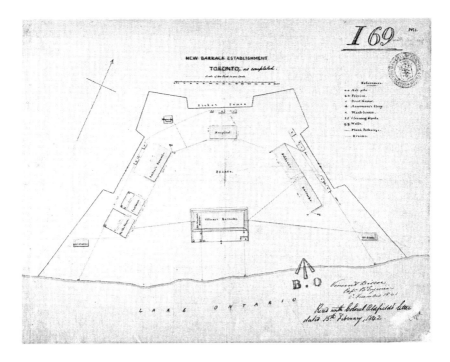

"*New Barrack Establishment, Toronto, as Completed*" *by Captain Vincent Biscoe of the Royal Engineers, December 2, 1841. Consisting of six main stone buildings around a parade square and surrounded by an eight-foot-high cedar picket fence, Toronto's New Fort was often described as "star-shaped." (To see the location of the New Fort in relation to the Old Fort that it was intended to replace, see map on page 36.*

Vincent Biscoe, "New Barrack Establishment, Toronto, as Completed," [December 2, 1841], Library and Archives Canada, NMC 5394.

town. An area extending 300 yards (approximately 275 metres) from the picket fence around the fort and from the shoreline was reserved for future military works, preventing this part of the military reserve from being leased or sold. Inside the enclosure, plank pathways connected the buildings in a circular route, enclosing the parade ground in the centre of the fort.

Thomas Glegg was a Royal Engineer stationed in Canada during the years 1840 and 1841. He was also a talented artist, who created a pictorial record of his travels and duty stations in a sketchbook. While in Toronto, Glegg drew a sketch of the newly constructed fort. "The whole is well drained," he wrote, "& is surrounded by a picket fence 8 feet high. As a Barrack it is complete in every respect having very desirable accommodation." Glegg was not the only one impressed with the New Fort. An American military officer, sent north to report on the state of Canada's military defences, was notably awed by the new barracks. Although the New Fort was still under construction when he observed it in late 1840, he noted of the new barracks that:

> [F]rom their position and arrangement they will be capable of considerable defence.... The walls are all of excellent masonry, three feet in thickness. The outside fronts of all the buildings have windows grated with strong iron bars to overlook the country. The enclosure of the barrack yard on all sides (except that of the lake) is a strong stockade composed of a double row of pickets, closely set and breaking joints. The pickets are each nine inches or a foot in diameter; they are secured by iron bolts to a square timber let in between the rows near the top. The stockade has loopholes throughout, but no ditch. Its gates are of oak, about six inches thick, with loopholes.[13]

Once the fort was completed, additions and alterations were made as necessary, many of them to accommodate the weather and climate of Toronto. For one thing, frequent wet weather was making the soil and clay road that led from the Old Fort to the new barracks impassable, and in December 1841 a proposal was made to macadamize the road, all the way from the picket fence surrounding the Old Fort, through the stockade fence surrounding the New Fort, and to the archway in the centre of Soldiers' Barracks Range No. 1 that marked the entranceway to the New Fort — a distance of 2,779 feet in total. Rain was also having a damaging effect on the parade square in the middle of the New Fort: "The whole of the present surface of the area within the Barrack Enclosure is formed of the natural soil, which is a very stiff yellow clay

The British Period (1840–1870)

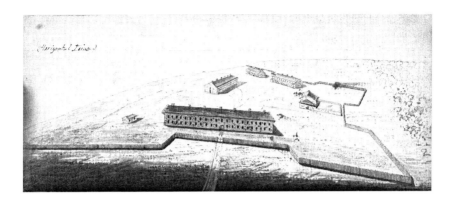

"Bird's Eye View of the New Fort at Toronto, Upper Canada, ca. 1841." This sketch by Lieutenant Thomas Glegg of the Royal Engineers, completed shortly after the construction of the New Fort, shows the fort from the main (east) entrance. The archway through Range No. 1 of the soldiers' barracks that led to the main parade square in the centre of the fort can be seen in the forefront.

Thomas Glegg Fonds, F 596, Archives of Ontario.

and which renders the Barrack Square unpassable in wet weather, the carts and wagons cut it up so much whilst in a moist state that its usefulness as a parade is much deteriorated when it is dry...." It was decided to cover the square with a thick layer of gravel, over an even thicker layer of broken stones, in an attempt to create a smooth surface suitable for soldiers to parade upon. An additional proposed improvement was to pave the surface drains with "the Lake Stone of the neighbourhood," as these drains were currently "formed of the natural soil and are of course very imperfect, and easily rendered useless by the passage of Cart Horses over them, indeed the constant rain alone in the Fall and Spring would have this effect upon them."[14]

Under the recommendation of the lieutenant-general commanding in Canada, it was decided in 1842 to construct fives courts and cricket grounds for the use of the troops where practicable at the principal military posts in Canada. As the Canadian climate necessitated a roofed fives courts, it was felt that such buildings would also be useful for more practical purposes in inclement weather. Consequently, plans and estimates were drawn up for the construction of a covered fives court within the New Fort grounds, to be located in the southeast corner next to the stables, and for the formation of a cricket ground on the adjoining military reserve. However, neither the fives court nor the cricket ground appear on any subsequent plans or maps of the New Fort; it appears that they were never built.[15]

An 1852 plan of the "New Stone Barrack Establishment" shows that a few additional improvements had, in fact, been made to the New Fort since 1841: a woodhouse had been constructed, as well as an exercising shed for prisoners. Also evident are improvements in the water system.[16]

The water supply to the New Fort proved to be a major and persistent problem. Captain Vincent Biscoe of the Royal Engineers reported at the end of December 1841 that the three wells within the barracks enclosure simply did not supply an adequate amount of water for the number of troops that occupied them. The water in these three wells — located near Range No. 1, Range No. 2, and in the yard attached to the officers' quarters — was at a very low level and tended to be muddy, Biscoe reported: "[V]ery little water has lately been drawn from these Wells and that only for Boiling Potatoes. [T]he Men obtain Water from the Lake for the purposes of Washing and Cooking in general, and the Officers Mess Kitchen is necessarily Supplied with water from the same place." Biscoe recommended the construction of a reservoir, which would be supplied by water brought in from the lake via an underground pipe, with a filter to purify the water. A system of this sort, Biscoe pointed out, would have added benefits in the case of a fire, "the water in the Lake being distant and difficult of access during the Winter and even during the other Seasons of the Year whenever there is a freeze." Apparently nothing was done, as a few months later, there were additional complaints about the water situation from Lieutenant-Colonel Spark, Commanding Officer of the 93rd Highlanders, who had moved from the Old Fort to the New Fort upon its completion. In the spring of 1842, Spark complained that the wells within the new garrison were not providing an adequate water supply. To make matters worse, clean water was not easily available at the lakeshore, thanks to four drains on the lakefront, which emptied refuse from the fort's cookhouse and privies into the water. As a result, clean water for cooking and drinking could only be obtained at a distance from the shore. To get usable water from the lake, one had to walk out to the end of a wooden wharf, where the water was "frequently discoloured with mud," but still of better quality. The wharf, however, was private property, and the owner had plans to move it to another location.[17]

Something had to be done about the water supply. By mid-1842, there were already 320 men stationed in the New Fort; Biscoe calculated that each man required three-and-a-half gallons of water per day. One temporary solution offered was to instruct the Commissariat Department to provide the supply of water required to the New Fort, until a more suitable solution was reached.[18]

Plans of the garrison from 1852 reveal that the water situation was finally improved through the construction of the "New Garrison Wharf," and a filter, from which water was brought to a tank and well-house located immediately east of the officers' quarters.

A BRITISH GARRISON: LIFE IN THE NEW FORT

Even after the rebellion crisis had passed, the political situation in Canada and relations with the United States remained tense. Events such as the 1838 Maine–New Brunswick boundary dispute — which nearly led to full-scale war as militiamen from both sides faced off — and further disputes between Britain and the United States over the determination of the Oregon boundary in the mid-1840s all served to reinforce the British government's dedication to maintaining British garrisons in Canada.

Of Britain's many colonial garrison towns during the mid-nineteenth century, Toronto was the favourite of many British officers. Lieutenant Arthur H. Freeling of the Royal Engineers spent fifteen months at Toronto, and considered it to be "the best quarter in Canada." Lieutenant-Colonel Sir James E. Alexander, in Toronto in the early 1850s, disliked the extremes of climate in Toronto, but in all other respects he praised the city. "And when we walk through its streets," he wrote, "and see its handsome stores, filled with choice goods from Europe and the States, and observe the business air of the well-dressed inhabitants, the good horses and vehicles moving actively about; we cannot be surprised to hear that property has increased enormously in value here, and that labour is in great request … education is carefully attended to.… The fertile soil of the back country, with thriving farms up Young [sic] Street (or road) &c., may have been the chief cause of the rapid growth of this fine city.…"[19] Toronto had grown considerably since 1793, boasting a population of thirty thousand by the early 1850s, and it continued to expand rapidly. From the first, the presence of a garrison had made possible the existence of a town at Toronto. In the following years, although the strength of the garrison varied according to the state of international relations, it continued to play an important role in the development and life of the city.

The presence of a garrison was considered to be an asset to the social and intellectual life of a community, and the presence of red-coated officers was highly desirable at local parties and other social events. Their popularity can be accounted for by the fact that most British officers were considered to be highly educated, cultured men, who were interested in books and music, and could be counted upon to provide worldly and stimulating conversation. The officers helped to promote such activities as theatre, game-hunting, fox-hunting, and cricket in the community. They provided regimental bands for concerts and dances, and staged colourful military parades and reviews. Furthermore, they tended to have more leisure time than the local businessmen, and consequently were more often available to serve as escorts at afternoon tea parties.[20]

Toronto was already regarded as a leading city in British North America. William Mackenzie, a British Army surgeon who was in Canada from 1839 to 1843, noted in his diary his pleasure at "remaining in a civilized place like the capital of Upper Canada" when he found himself stationed at Toronto in 1839. In his diary, Mackenzie recorded the 93rd Regiment's involvement with the city of Toronto: the regimental band performed at balls and dances; members of the regiment participated in public athletic competitions; and large crowds of Torontonians turned out to watch the military reviews held on Garrison Common. Mackenzie also remarked on the popularity of the members of the 93rd as party guests, "'to add Brilliancy to the scene,' as they say of the Redcoats." Somewhat reclusive at first, within a few months of his arrival at Toronto, Dr. Mackenzie became acquainted with some of the principal families of the city, and often accompanied the young ladies of these families on rides through the neighbourhood.[21]

While Torontonians regarded the redcoats as a welcome addition to their social functions, the officers of the garrison enjoyed taking part in local social events, which tended to be less formal than at their home stations in Britain. Lieutenant Freeling, upon his departure from Toronto in April of 1842, remarked that in Toronto "the society is perhaps the best in Canada and I individually have had great kindness shown to me."[22]

Not only did the presence of smartly dressed British officers add glamour to local society and social functions, but they were also regarded as highly desirable marriage material for Canadian ladies. "Town-garrison" weddings were few, however, because while such a marriage may have been considered an opportunity for social advancement by the locals, the officers probably saw it as a social error. More practically, often a young British officer needed a wealthy wife to support him.[23] This side of the situation did not escape Dr. Mackenzie. While he enjoyed Toronto society, he also remained somewhat cynical: "As for the inhabitants [of Toronto] they fancy themselves very aristocratic, there are [*sic*], as in all provincial Towns, lots of scandal, & every body [*sic*] knows what his neighbour eats, drinks & wishes for. But notwithstanding, I think there are some very nice families here; there are certainly many very ladylike handsome Girls, already I believe to accept of a red coat, with other very ordinary pretensions, but alas! the Sweet fair ones are all minus the needful!"[24]

Gilbert Elliot, a subaltern in the Rifle Brigade, came to Toronto in 1847 at the age of twenty-one, and was stationed at the New Fort until 1850. He maintained a journal which, along with the letters he wrote home to his family, paints a vivid picture of the life of a young British officer in Toronto during the mid-nineteenth century. Elliot hailed from a distinguished lineage: the Elliots of Roxburghshire in Scotland. His father was the Second Earl of Minto; his brother-in-law, Lord John Russell, was the prime minister of Britain and leader of the Whig Party; and Elliot's nephew, the 4th Earl of Minto, would become the governor general of Canada in 1898.

Flustered by sudden orders to move to Toronto in August of 1847, after just having settled in at Montreal, Elliot initially viewed his Toronto posting with apprehension. Stoically, he made up his mind to like Toronto, and two months later was able to admit that he was, in fact, enjoying his new station: "It is generally the fashion in the army to abuse every place you are quartered in," he wrote in a letter to his mother; "I am happy to say I am very unfashionable."[25]

Elliot was soon enjoying Toronto society. He found the locals to be prone to gossip, yet quite interesting and lively — unlike his military duties, which he described as monotonous and occasionally trying. He quickly discovered the popularity of a British officer at a party, and took advantage of this. He reported to his family that, "Toronto is certainly the gayest place that I ever saw, and I have myself been dissipating at a great rate during the last fortnight at balls, tea fights, dinners and breakfasts, and am engaged three deep for a fortnight to come, the fact is, the people are beginning to find out what a nice young man I am, and how useful I am at small tea parties." Elliot's letters also contain descriptions of cricket games, fishing, and game-hunting on the Common, as well as parties and picnics organized by the Rifle Brigade for the townspeople. These were always very popular events. One picnic given by the Rifle Brigade's officers and featuring dancing to the regimental band was attended by seventy-five Torontonians.[26]

Elliot's letters and journal also provide a picture of life in the newly built barracks at Toronto. He liked the fact that the New Fort was located at a bit of a distance from the town itself; this was probably preferable to being quartered in the town. In any case, the garrison's location, west of the town and the Old Fort, provided easy access to Garrison Common, which abounded with wildlife for game-hunting, and to Lake Ontario, which offered opportunities for fishing and boating. Elliot reported that some mornings he could actually see the foam and spray of Niagara Falls from his window.[27]

In the winter, the lake became a centre of amusement for both the members of the garrison and the townspeople. Elliot wrote:

> Last week we had great fun on the ice when all the ladies made their appearance, some skating and the others walking, the walkers all expected to be pulled about the

ice on small sleighs by the gentlemen, I succeeded in upsetting more of the fair sex than most people; it was a most absurd sight to see the whole ice covered with little bits of sleighs containing one or two ladies with two men harnessed to them; the great object seemed, to upset them as often as possible by turning suddenly to one side and shooting them out there must have been a great many sore bones among them.

According to Elliot, "all Toronto" turned out for "all kinds of fun" when the bay froze over, and occasionally the whole lake froze over. On

"Sleigh Scene, Toronto Bay," 1842 or 1843, painted by J.T. Downman and lithographed by E. Walker. Like Gilbert Elliot of the Rifle Brigade, who was stationed at Stanley Barracks from 1847 to 1850, Torontonians enjoyed sleighing on the bay when it froze over, as depicted in this lithograph. The artist, J.T. Downman, was a lieutenant in the 83rd Regiment, and dedicated this print to the officers of the regiment, which was in Toronto from July 1842 until the spring of 1843. (The shore and buildings depicted are not accurate.)

Toronto Public Library (TRL), J. Ross Robertson Collection: JRR 311.

the few occasions that this occurred, some soldiers attempted to desert by crossing over the ice to the American shore — many of them were later found either frozen or drowned.[28]

Life at the Toronto garrison was evidently not as enjoyable for the enlisted men as it was for the officers. Desertion was a problem in all seasons, the American border being relatively close by, even by overland routes. Elliot was personally affected when his groom tried to desert, taking with him Elliot's horse, dog cart, and harness. And when six members of the Rifle Brigade's band deserted, taking their instruments with them, it was a great loss, not only because the band was ruined and it would be difficult to find six qualified musicians to replace them, but also because it was the officers themselves who financed the regimental band, and the stolen instruments had been purchased at their own personal expense.[29]

Although Royal Engineer Thomas Glegg may have referred to the New Fort as a very desirable accommodation when it was built, he himself never had the experience of living in the barracks through the course of a harsh Toronto winter. One cold January, Gilbert Elliot complained in a letter to his mother:

> The thermometer has been below zero for the last four days and I cannot get my bedroom warmer than 27° even with a stove in it, so that every morning it takes me about a quarter of an hour to thaw my sponges by pouring hot water upon them. I got both my precious little ears frostbitten but managed to bring them to life again by … a great deal of rubbing. If the Engineers could only be quartered in these barracks for a short time in the winter there might be a chance of getting the rooms a little warmer.

On such days, the barracks were so cold that, at mess, the water in the officers' finger glasses would be frozen at dinnertime.[30]

The cold winters in Toronto also proved expensive for young officers, as they had to purchase a great deal of winter clothing. Elliot kept

The British Period (1840–1870)

"Barracks, 29th July 1848, Canada." Unknown artist. This previously unpublished early drawing of the New Fort was recently discovered in a private family collection in Australia, and was very likely sketched by an officer or soldier stationed at the barracks in the 1840s.

Courtesy of Allan Mortimer.

two servants, whom he also had to supply with appropriate winter wear. Other expenses included the cost of the horse Elliot purchased, and mess fees. It is not very surprising that an officer in such circumstances would consider only a marriage that would better his financial situation. While Elliot enjoyed the relative informality of Canadian etiquette, and what he considered to be the absence of prudery in Canadian ladies (perhaps less refined than their English counterparts, he noted, but "very good fellows all the same"), he also realized that some of them were "baits laid to catch unwary soldiers."[31]

Back home in Scotland, Elliot's family worried that Gilbert might "take the bait" himself. He assured his concerned relatives that "you need not be affraid [sic] of my getting married. I am not so green, for tho' the ladies of Toronto are very charming, money is a thing which tho' often talked about is seldom seen in Canada, & it is absolutely necessary that the gal of my heart should possess it." Yet despite his confident reassurances, Elliot in fact courted and became engaged to a Canadian, Miss Jane Fitzgerald. His father refused them permission to marry, claiming that he did not have enough money to support both his son and his son's wife, and going so far as to arrange a six-month leave of absence for his son to come home and take his mind off Miss Fitzgerald. Elliot eventually, and regretfully, gave in to his father's wishes.[32]

In addition to their role in the social life of Toronto, the members of the garrison provided some more practical services. The troops were often called upon to help put out fires in the city. Elliot detested this duty, which could involve calls in the middle of the night, and having to run all the way to the town, sometimes through deep snow. His chief complaint, however, when it came to firefighting duty, was against the people of Toronto. Each time Elliot and his men were called to a fire, upon their arrival at the scene the townspeople let them do all the firefighting, even if their own homes and property were in danger from the blaze. On one occasion, the townspeople completely left the firefighting to the soldiers, while they themselves headed to the public houses to drink! Elliot ascribed this to simple laziness on the part of Torontonians.[33]

In the absence of a large police force in the city, the local garrison was sometimes called upon to act in aid of the civil power, generally an unpopular duty with soldiers. In 1849, Toronto was the scene of constant rioting, as the local Tory population protested the Rebellion Losses Bill, which had been passed by the Canadian legislature to compensate those who had suffered losses as a result of the 1837–38 rebellions. Governor General Lord Elgin, who had signed the bill into law, was burned in effigy. The rioting was so intense that it provoked fears of another rebellion. During this unrest, the Rifle Brigade took its turn policing the situation. "We have been called out two or three times," wrote Gilbert Elliot, "but have never had to act, & I hope never shall, as it is the most unpleasant duty soldiers can be put to; The Loyalists about here are very strong so of course there will be few people to act as militia in case of a row.…"[34]

In July 1851, troops were called out to clear the streets when a "considerable riot" broke out in response to an Anti-Clergy Reserve meeting held at St. Lawrence Hall. The military was summoned only after the mayor had been struck down by a hurled stone, and after police had been "also severely handled" by the riotous crowd. Obviously Toronto's police force was too small to handle large disturbances, making the presence of the garrison a decided advantage to City authorities. However, the troops and local law keepers did not always work together harmoniously. The Journal of the High Bailiff for 1849, for example, records that on June 8 of that year, three Toronto police constables "proceeded to the Garrison Commons, by order of Ald. Thos. Bell to remove some disorderly characters, when they were brutally assaulted and beaten by soldiers of the Rifle Brigade." 1849 is the first year for which the High Bailiff (later called the Chief Constable) began providing detailed summaries of the activities of Toronto's fledgling police force. These accounts reveal that the Garrison Common was one of the most frequently patrolled areas of Toronto by constables in search of "disorderly characters." Most of these patrols resulted in the arrest of several prisoners. The fact that most of the "disorderly characters" apprehended, according to these reports, were women, suggests that they were very likely prostitutes, and may explain the Rifle Brigade's defence of them.[35]

Overall, however, Toronto loved its garrison. When news was received that the Rifle Brigade was to be sent from Toronto to a new posting, City Council expressed a "civic farewell" to the officers and men of the regiment, praising the "gentlemanly deportment and urbanity of the Officers and the steady and orderly conduct of the Men" during their stay in Toronto, and thanking them for their "ready and effective assistance" to the civil authorities in the fighting of fires, the protection of property, and the preservation of order.[36] Clearly, Britain's colonial garrisons, such as the one in Toronto, were seen as performing two distinct roles: the prevention of foreign invasions, and the prevention of domestic disturbances. This dual role made the presence, as well as the continued strength, of the garrisons all the more important. A report from the deputy quartermaster general's office in 1847 warned against the removal of troops from garrison duty in Canada, one of the main objections to removal being that "The garrisons are so weak that, on any sudden call for troops to be detached, say, at elections, riots, and suchlike, the posts are left too lightly held."[37]

Not everyone appreciated the continued presence and influence of British garrisons in Canada. Lord Elgin pointed out in 1847 that the colonists could not help but regard the British military force with some jealousy, feeling that it was maintained for the benefit of imperial, and not colonial, interests.[38] Many Canadians clung to the mistaken belief that it was the Canadian militia, not the British regulars, who were responsible for the successful defence of Canada from the invading American forces in 1812, and resented the presence of the redcoats. George T. Denison, a prominent Toronto citizen whose family boasted a long military tradition, recalled hearing bugle calls from the New Fort as a child; he was constantly aware of the presence of British regulars stationed there, particularly during the years 1846 to 1854. Denison (who was later to command the Governor General's Body Guard, organized by his grandfather in 1822), believed that the presence of the regulars had a negative effect on the local militia. "The presence of a British regiment in good condition, and splendidly maintained and drilled," he wrote in his 1901 memoirs, *Soldiering in Canada*, "rendered it impossible for a militia corps self-supported to compete either in numbers, equipment or drill,

"Old Fort from Common, 19th July 1848." Unknown artist. *The same anonymous artist who sketched the New Fort in July 1848 also took the opportunity to record the appearance of Fort York in his sketchbook at around the same time.*

Courtesy of Allan Mortimer.

and, naturally, comparisons were drawn much to the disadvantage of the latter. The men used to be laughed at and ridiculed to such an extent, that it was found much more pleasant to keep out of sight as much as possible, and to avoid attracting any attention."[39] Clearly, however, this "splendidly maintained and drilled" army exercised a positive influence, if only indirectly, by providing a model and setting standards for the militia.

By the 1840s, the military reserve designated by Simcoe in 1793 had shrunk considerably. The expansion of Toronto had gradually shifted the eastern boundary of the ordnance lands from Peter Street to Garrison Creek (just east of the Old Fort), reducing the area of the reserve to approximately half of its original size. About twelve hectares, or thirty acres, of land in the northern portion of the reserve was granted by the military to the province for a lunatic asylum in 1845. Smaller lots were leased to individuals. In 1845, Mayor William H. Boulton requested that the City be allowed to occupy the land remaining in the garrison reserve after the lunatic asylum grant had been transacted, proposing to turn the reserve into a public park, enclosed by a carriage drive. Boulton insisted that the military would in fact benefit from this arrangement: the City would build a good, macadamized road to Lot Street, and in addition, "by the vigilance of the Civic Authorities the Garrison would be relieved from the numerous worthless characters who are continually infesting the Barracks." The proposed park apparently did not materialize, as later maps of the reserve do not indicate a park, nor the accompanying road and carriage drive. Some of the reserve was, however, donated to the City. Most of the land simply became known as the "Common," and part of it was temporarily transferred to the Militia Department for the use of Toronto volunteers as a rifle range.[40]

The Provincial Agricultural Association also sought a piece of the Garrison Common land. The Association had been formed in 1846 to bring together the province's leading agriculturalists and manufacturers and to provide a showplace for their products, in the form of a provincial fair. The fair was held in a different city each year. Toronto won the opportunity to host the fair in the years 1846 and 1852, and the Association used tents and temporary wooden buildings to house the exhibits and events of the fair. For the upcoming 1859 fair in Toronto,

STANLEY BARRACKS

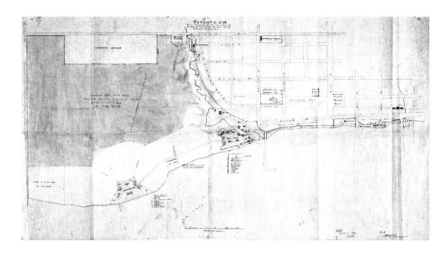

"Toronto, C.W. — Plan to accompany the Returns called for by Board's order dated 10th June 1851." This map by Lieutenant A.R. Vyvyan Crease of the Royal Engineers shows the military reserve and the position of the New Fort in relation to the Old Fort, which it was built to replace.

Library and Archives Canada, C-137339.

however, a new, more suitable — and more permanent — site was desired. City Council, after lengthy negotiations with military officials, obtained a portion of the garrison reserve. This land consisted of eight hectares (approximately twenty acres) located immediately south of the Provincial Lunatic Asylum. It was here that Toronto's first permanent exhibition building was erected — the "Palace of Industry." A one-storey building in the form of a cross, it was enclosed in glass and became known as the "Crystal Palace," an imitation of the famous Crystal Palace constructed at Hyde Park in England for the 1851 London Exposition — the first World's Fair. The 1859 fair at Toronto, which took place September 28 through October 1, attracted many members of the local garrison, for whom the twenty-five-cent admission fee was waived, providing that the men were in uniform and in the charge of a non-commissioned officer, and that no more than fifty were admitted at one time.[41]

Britain drastically reduced its garrisons in Canada in 1854, when troops were needed in the Crimean War. British regulars returned in force,

The British Period (1840–1870)

however, by the early 1860s, when United States–Canada tensions created by the American Civil War — in particular, the seizure of *Trent*, a neutral British ship, by the Union Navy to remove two Confederate agents heading to London and Paris to seek European support for the Confederate cause — and raids by United States–based Fenians into Canadian territory, made the defence of British North America a major priority and concern once again. Many suspected that the United States was ready to invade Canada, whether it be to finally fulfill its objective of 1812, or simply to keep the Federal Army occupied once the Civil War had ended.[42] Twelve hundred British regulars were sent to Toronto; as the proposed defensive works for the New Fort had not been built, Fort York was re-armed and became Toronto's primary harbour defence until the 1880s.[43]

W. Howard Russell, an Englishman travelling through the United States and Canada in 1862, reported messing daily with the officers of the 30th Regiment while he was in Toronto, where, "They were quartered in a substantial old-fashioned barrack on the shore of Lake Ontario … surrounded by an earthen parapet with traverses and embrasures." He held little regard for the usefulness of the Old Fort as a defensive structure, however, stating: "No more uncomfortable place could well be imagined in the face of an enemy. The defences are so ludicrous that a Chinese engineer would despise them. Certainly, we have no right to laugh at Americans … if we take one glance at the fortifications of Toronto." In his report on the defences of Canada, Russell recommended the construction of fortifications on the site of the new barracks.[44]

In approximately 1860, a military cemetery was established between the Old and New Forts. The inscriptions on the grave markers erected there during the 1860s reveal which regiments were stationed at Toronto at that time. They included the Royal Canadian Rifles, the 13th Hussars, the 16th Regiment, the 30th Regiment, and the 47th Regiment. Most of the grave markers were erected by fellow soldiers. An unusually high proportion of the soldiers who were buried in this cemetery in the 1860s were the victims of drowning in Lake Ontario. Some wives and children of soldiers were interred here, as well.[45]

Apparently, there was a shortage of quarters at this time, as several buildings again were leased as barracks. The 13th Hussars were quartered

STANLEY BARRACKS

"Crystal Palace, King St., Toronto, erected 1857 (used as Provincial Exhibition space, and after 1866 as 13th Hussars Barracks)." Photo by Octavius Thompson, 1867. After a portion of the garrison reserve was obtained from the military by City officials for provincial exhibition purposes, the Palace of Industry or, as it was more commonly known, the "Crystal Palace," was built. It was Toronto's first permanent exhibition building, but would also occasionally be used for military purposes, including the housing of troops when barracks space was in short supply.

Octavius Thompson Fonds, F 4356-0-0-0-39, Archives of Ontario.

in the Crystal Palace, which the Department of Militia and Defence rented from the City.[46]

The Royal Artillery was stationed at the New Fort in the 1860s. Artilleryman Lieutenant Harry E. Baines kept a diary in which he described departing from the New Fort on August 3, 1863, along with two other officers, for a month's cruise on Lake Ontario in his yacht *Breeze* — and

The British Period (1840–1870)

"New Fort, Toronto" by Henry Egerton Baines, July 10, 1863. Baines joined the British army as an artillery lieutenant in the early 1860s, and served in Canada from 1861 onwards. In 1863, along with some fellow officers, he took a month's leave and sailed around Lake Ontario on board a ship named Breeze. This watercolour is one of the illustrations Baines included in the journal he kept of his voyage, which he entitled "The Cruise of the Breeze." Baines was later stationed in Quebec City, where he assisted in rescue efforts during the huge fire that occurred on October 14, 1866 — a fire that destroyed over two thousand buildings and left over eighteen thousand people homeless. Baines died from injuries he sustained during the fire.

Henry Egerton Baines, Henry Egerton Baines Fonds, Library and Archives Canada, accession number 1995-37-4, R 12032-2-4-E.

engaging in some unofficial "spying" on American towns along the way. Baines's diary also includes a watercolour he painted of the New Fort.[47]

During the 1860s, when the Royal Artillery was stationed at Toronto, additional stabling was built at the New Fort for 250 horses. Plans of the barracks show that a large area of land directly north of the fort was enclosed, and Royal Artillery stables were built there. The new stables were not the only alteration required for the New Fort. A report on the condition of Toronto's military works, completed in October 1863, provides some interesting details about the living conditions at the New Fort at the time. There were no special married quarters, and married soldiers had to stay in ordinary barrack rooms. The rooms' occupants relied on stoves for warmth, and candles for light. The lavatory consisted of a small brick building divided into three compartments: an ablutions room, a bath fitted with two iron baths for men, and a laundry fitted with two boilers and a bath for women. The kitchen was outfitted with boilers and an oven, with ventilation provided by small openings in the walls near the ceilings. The New Fort's hospital was a brick building, complete with a surgery and a dead-house; it was reported to be in good repair, and, with a capacity to take in twenty-four patients at one time, the hospital sufficiently met the requirements of the garrison. The report also listed a number of new buildings that had sprung up within the New Fort, including two shoeing shops, a tailor's shop, an armourer's shop, a collar maker's shop, a farrier's shop, and a wheeler's shop. The huge new stables, built for the arrival of troops from England in 1861, were noted. Other new additions mentioned include a library room and a skittle alley.[48] "From the rapid inspection taken of these New Barracks and from Reports received it would appear that they are on the whole as good and well provided with necessary offices &c as any Barracks in Canada. The Barrack rooms are constructed the entire width of the building with windows at both ends so that they obtain a thorough draft from end to end." The October 1863 report noted that approximately 18 officers and 234 other ranks were stationed in the New Fort.[49]

 The Toronto garrison was at a peak in the 1860s. Another Royal Artillery lieutenant, Francis Duncan, who saw six years' service in North America, was in Toronto in the early 1860s and referred to it as a "bustling and wealthy city," which, as a military quarter, was much liked. W. Howard Russell was favourably impressed by the hospitality and camaraderie among the officers, and was pleased to find that the number of desertions at this time was low.[50] Occasionally, the officers of the garrison held "amateur theatricals" at the New Fort, and invited the general public to attend.[51]

The British Period (1840–1870)

Canadians' military enthusiasm, and consequently the strength and development of the local militia, rose and fell according to the state of international relations. With the reduction of British troops in Canada to provide troops for Crimea, Canadians' enthusiasm had led the Canadian government to pass the Militia Act of 1855, authorizing a five-thousand-man "Volunteer Force." Public interest declined after the Crimean crisis, and increased again with the 1860s Canada–United States crises. British regulars served as models and instructors for the militia, and during the 1860s, as part of general militia reform, schools of instruction for militia officers were established in Toronto and Quebec. The Toronto military school was held in the New Fort. One of the students was William D. Otter of the Queen's Own Rifles Battalion. The military schools offered training courses of no more than three months' duration, consisting of drill, military law, and administration. This was strictly an elementary training course; for more advanced professional training, officers were sent to Great Britain.[52]

On June 14 and 16, 1869, 256 men, 29 women, and 44 children of the 1st Battalion, 60th Royal Rifles, arrived at Toronto by steamer in two detachments from Montreal. They went into quarters in the Old and New Forts, and occupied both until September 28, when the entire detachment (with the exception of a few officers, the hospital establishment, and a few married families) moved into the Old Fort, leaving the New Fort occupied almost entirely by Royal Artillery men. The annual report of the 60th Rifles detachment stationed at Toronto contained a description of the New Fort, as it appeared in 1869: the large two-storied stone buildings, forming "an irregular parallelogram," on a barrack square. The report noted:

> Each block of houses is detached from the others, admitting of a free transit of air in every direction. In addition to a square of one storied huts, which comprises the Artillery Stables and adjoins the Barrack Yard on the North, on its South and East aspects, of recent years, four large well ventilated wooden houses have been erected, which can well accommodate 20 married

families and 90 men. The entire is enclosed by a quadrangular loopholed Stockade, and is situated about one mile from Toronto, close to the Lake on the open Common already alluded to; and which is used for a musketry practice and General parade ground during the summer season.

As for the interior living conditions: "The rooms are lofty, heated with stoves, and lighted with candles, or (at the men's own expense) coal oil. They are arranged in sets of two, with staircases intervening.… The site is open and exposed, and overlooks the Lake on the South, and the Common on the North, East, and West; and enjoys an elevation of about 10 feet above the lake's surface and 245 feet above the level of the Sea." The report notes that the water supply is drawn up from the lake through use of a filter pump, and is then distributed by means of a cart. The only complaint registered concerned the sewage system, the latrines being located over the sewers, which drained their contents into the lake, close to the officers' quarters, not far from where water was procured for use by the fort's residents.

The report also discusses the ramifications of the extremes of temperature experienced during a typical year in Toronto. The men's uniforms had proven to be too hot and heavy during the summer, when Toronto's temperatures often reached ninety degrees Fahrenheit (32 degrees Celsius) in the shade, and the forage caps the soldiers wore did not protect their heads sufficiently from the sun. The report recommended that the men be allowed to keep their beards during the summer months, rather than being required to shave at winter's end:

> Summer's heat and Winter's cold extend to great limits; and Spring and Autumn are extremely variable; that temperatures often alter 20 degrees in as many hours; but with each variable spring comes the order for the removal of Comforters and the Winter's growth of

Beard; leaving the throat entirely exposed to the deleterious [sic] influence of the well known vicissitudes of weather which exist at this season.... *Permanent beards* would undoubtedly in this climate be highly beneficial to the health of the men at all *seasons of the year.*"

The removal of the protective layer of hair on the chin, cheeks, and throat, the report suggests, may have been responsible for the increased number of respiratory diseases, particularly tonsillitis, among the men.[53]

As the decade drew to a close, however, the role of the British regulars in Canada was coming to an end. The Red River Expedition of 1870 has been described by Canadian military historian George F.G. Stanley as the "last British military operation in North America." In the spring of that year, two rifle battalions, comprised of seven hundred militiamen, were recruited in Ontario and Quebec, as the Canadian component of the Red River force being dispatched to Manitoba to confront Metis resistance under Louis Riel. Before being sent west, the recruits were gathered in Toronto and housed at the Crystal Palace on the garrison reserve, where they underwent basic training. The recruits at the Crystal Palace complained about the quality of rations and about bedbug infestations. Several found themselves incarcerated in the guardroom for fighting, or for breaking curfew. Nevertheless, they were turned into full-time soldiers, and in May, after a parade and inspection, they travelled by train to Collingwood to embark on a steamer bound for the West.[54]

As was often the case, the building required some repairs after its military occupation. The costs for damages to the Crystal Palace were charged to the militia and the City began the necessary work to ready the building for the upcoming annual meeting of the Agricultural Association that would take place in the Crystal Palace that fall.[55]

STANLEY BARRACKS

THE WITHDRAWAL OF BRITISH FORCES FROM CANADA

In 1870, an era came to an end as Britain decided to withdraw its troops from Canada. This decision was the result of many factors and trends that had been developing over the course of the past decade. For many Britons, the events taking place on the European continent took precedence over Canadian concerns; developing European conflicts, such as that between France and Prussia in 1870, made a larger home force a necessity. There was a desire to avoid another war on two fronts — Europe and North America. Also playing a significant role was a developing philosophy of decentralization of the Empire. Not everyone regarded colonies in the well-being of the nation as important as they had once been. For many British taxpayers, the issue for years had been simply a financial one: they were tired of paying for Canada's defence. Canada, now a confederated Dominion, should play a greater role in her own defence. Britain also realized its vulnerability in North America. While the United States was considered to be the only viable threat to Canada, it was a daunting one. The United States had duly demonstrated its military strength during its recent civil war. The land defensibility of Canada, in the face of a potential invasion by American forces, was doubtful. Britain's preferred strategy in the 1870s was to withdraw its troops from the colonies, build up the home garrisons, and maintain a Canadian garrison only at Halifax, for British North American defence now rested in British sea power, or, preferably, in peaceful negotiations with the United States to settle differences before they had the chance to rise to the level of armed conflict. This attitude — based on the principle that an "undefended border" was the best solution — was confirmed by the 1871 Treaty of Washington, an attempt to peacefully settle by negotiation outstanding issues between Britain and the United States that had arisen during the Civil War period.

Britain did not suggest that it would no longer defend Canada in times of crisis, or that it was severing the imperial bond. In fact, while the presence of British redcoats in Canada had served as a tangible symbol of ties with the mother country, it was hoped that the withdrawal of the British military presence would in fact increase imperial unity by lessening the financial burden of British taxpayers for colonial defence, thereby ending a major cause of anti-colonial feeling in Britain.

The last British garrison (with the exception of Halifax) left Canada in the fall of 1871. Ordnance buildings and lands were transferred to the government of Canada. In Toronto, the British troops who had been quartered in the New Fort had moved out by the end of June 1870. All that remained was to officially turn over the fort to the Dominion government. Per instructions from the minister of militia and defence, Colonel R.G. Hamilton, commanding officer of the Royal Engineers, left his Montreal office on Thursday morning, July 14, to catch a train to Toronto. In the meantime, Lieutenant-Colonel Thomas Wily, director of stores, was heading to Toronto from Ottawa. The next day, the two proceeded to the New Fort, where Wily formally received the grounds and buildings of the New Fort from Hamilton. After an inspection of the premises, however, Wily reported to the minister of militia and urged the immediate appointment of a caretaker for the fort:

> When taking over the Buildings, I found out, that a forcible entry had been effected therein, & that they had been occupied during the night previous, by some loose, & disorderly women, to their manifest danger & detriment. I directed Major Goodwin, the Storekeeper, to place himself in communication with the Police Authorities of Toronto, & the result was, that on the following day, seven women, & one man, were arrested on the premises, & committed to gaol for a term of three months, as vagabonds.

In the meantime, Wily temporarily appointed Goodwin as caretaker.[56]

On September 26, the transfer at Toronto was completed as Wily took over the Old Fort and adjoining lands. Again, Wily expressed some concerns over the condition of the property. Both the Old and New Forts, Wily reported, "were suffering delapidation [sic] and injury, from the hands of the loose & disorderly characters in the habit of frequenting those places." Wily also reported finding several military families occupying barracks rooms (some of them families of troops who were away on the Red River Expedition). The families were allowed to stay, and live-in caretakers were hired to look after the property, in exchange for free quarters. The Department of Militia and Defence also took over the leases of those civilians who leased portions of Garrison Common.[57]

CHAPTER TWO

The Canadian Period (1870–1914)

THE DOMINION GOVERNMENT TAKES OVER THE NEW FORT

Suddenly in possession of the ordnance buildings and land at Toronto, Canada's Department of Militia and Defence found little immediate use for them, and aside from the presence of a few tenants and caretakers, the New Fort was neglected for several years. The buildings fell into disrepair, while the grounds around the fort were left uncared for.

Corporal Sam Steele, who had served in the Red River Expedition and had just completed a year-long course at the artillery school at Kingston, was sent to the New Fort in 1872 to put the artillery stores in order. He found "everything in the worst state of confusion, disorder, and neglect, in fact as bad as could be. The stores were piled in heaps on the floors.…" Steele and his men spent the next month straightening up the mess. Steele remained at the fort to train the Toronto garrison battery (a militia artillery unit) when they came into barracks for their annual training. When the course ended, the men's final evening in the New Fort barracks was celebrated with a smoking concert, during which Goodwin, the eighty-two-year-old military storekeeper, entertained with songs and jigs.[1]

There were other signs of life at the New Fort. The Toronto Volunteers' rifle practice and local rifle associations' annual matches continued to be held on the Garrison Common. When Casimir Gzowski, president of the

Ontario Rifle Association, asked for the use of a room in the New Fort for storage of tents, blankets, and targets, his request was refused by the Department of Militia and Defence. However, the Association was allowed use of the Officers' Mess room in the New Fort for administrative purposes during the few days of their upcoming annual prize meeting. The Department's refusal to give up a room for storage suggests that Ottawa recognized the military importance of the New Fort, and the report issued on the matter indicated plans for a possible military use of the fort in the near future: "to let them put their things in the New Barracks would be in many respects very objectionable, *departmentally speaking*, and we may want these Barracks as a Military School before long."[2]

A request from some Toronto gentlemen for the rental of the Garrison Common for the establishment of a Turf Club to race horses was also refused. Turf Club supporters promised that their activities would not interfere with rifle practice on the Common, but Gzowski, protesting on behalf of the Toronto militia volunteers and local rifle

"*Toronto — the Ontario Rifle Association Match — the All-Comers' Match: View Showing the Lunatic Asylum*" by P.W. Canning, 1874. The Ontario Rifle Association was only one of numerous groups seeking use of garrison reserve land for its activities, causing endless frustration on the part of military officials.

Canadian Illustrated News, Vol. X, September 19, 1874, 181, Library and Archives Canada, C-061433.

associations, disagreed. Robert B. Denison, acting deputy adjutant general of militia, concurred with Gzowski. Garrison Common, he pointed out, was the only suitable ground for rifle range purposes within several miles of Toronto, and should therefore continue to be used for range and drill purposes. Locating a race course adjacent to a military barracks was simply inadvisable. Furthermore, a request from the Ontario government to purchase the Old Fort was refused on the grounds that this would cut off the direct road from the town through the Old Fort to the New Fort and the rifle ranges.[3]

While possessively guarding its property in Toronto for future military use, the Department of Militia and Defence nevertheless neglected the forts. The New Fort was nominally in the charge of Major De la Cherois T. Irwin, who, as commandant of the School of Gunnery at Kingston, was hardly able to inspect personally, or effectively take command of, the Toronto buildings. Consequently, the Department had no record of the condition or occupancy of the New Fort. In February of 1874, Irwin asked to be relieved of this responsibility, and the Department placed the New Fort in the charge of the local storekeeper, Lieutenant-Colonel Goodwin. Goodwin was somewhat reluctant to take over these duties, unclear of where his authority and responsibilities lay, since he knew there were a number of squatters occupying the fort. Colonel Thomas Scoble was living in the New Fort without a lease, along with his family, and his two servant men and their families. Goodwin contacted Colonel Wily for clarification. He wanted to know who had authorized Scoble to inhabit the barracks. How should Goodwin proceed in dealing with these squatters?[4]

In response to Goodwin's concerns, in March, Lieutenant-Colonel Durie, the deputy adjutant general for Military District No. 2, inspected the New Fort in order to assess this unusual situation of unauthorized inhabitants. He was accompanied by Goodwin, as well as Sergeant George Crush, in charge of a detachment of "A" Battery, Royal Canadian Artillery, stationed at Toronto. Durie was soon able to report back to Ottawa that Colonel Scoble and his family were indeed occupying seven or eight rooms in the officers' quarters. The Scobles, along with their servants, had moved in last November by permission of Lieutenant-Colonel George A.

French, who at the time was commanding "A" Battery in Kingston.[5] Durie reported that Scoble was also using a large forage shed on the grounds as a storehouse, and had appropriated ten stalls in the officers' stables, in which he planned to house a pair of horses and a cow (although Durie found both the horses and the cow at large in the fort). Scoble was also using the Prison Drill Shed as a cattle shed, leaving the building, Durie noted, "in a very dirty condition." There were other tenants, as well, both civilian and military, occupying various buildings within the fort. James Langdon, who worked during the summers for the Ontario Rifle Association and wherever he could find work during the winters, was living there with his wife and family. Caretaker Henry O'Brien and his family had been residing in the part of the hospital building for several years. Durie also found two married men from "A" Battery: Gunner Scoefield and Gunner Clay. Scoefield, Durie reported, was nominally in charge of the fort — placed there by authority of Lieutenant-Colonel French — but, "Does not appear to exercise any Authority, What-Ever." None of these New Fort residents, however, would take responsibility for the fort or for the condition of the barracks. Durie expressed his concern over the situation: "I may be permitted to remark that it appears to me that to permit Gentlemen or others — *not directly Amenable* to Authority to reside within the New Fort is not Conducive, to the Public Service — or to the Preservation of Public Property."[6]

As for the general physical condition of the New Fort, Durie reported that part of the exterior picket fence around the fort had blown away, allowing free access to the fort, and needed repair as quickly as possible. Horses and cows were wandering throughout the grounds. "The Fort Generally and all the Buildings appertaining to it — out of order — Doors without Hinges — thrown down — Gates without Fastenings &c." Lieutenant-Colonel Goodwin submitted his own report regarding the condition of the New Fort: "The occupation of the Quarters I Consider nothing to what the Presence of So many Cows and Horses with Waggons … which must be Continually Passing in and out of the Fort which Causes the Gates to be Left Open always which makes the Fort a Common Thoroughfare.… Many Doors of These Sheds are Lying about and Broken of Their Hinges and Left to Rot.…" No one would take responsibility, he added. Scoble blamed the artillery men for the damage, who in turn blamed Scoble. "[T]here is no believing Either Parties," grumbled Goodwin. When he asked Sergeant Crush to account for the condition of the New Fort, Crush would only say that when the fort was handed over to his care in the fall of 1873 by two officers of the "A" Battery, he had "received no Inventory nor any document respecting a single article within the New Fort Buildings. I took it over by word of mouth in the following words, 'There is the New Fort.'" In spite of this chaos, Goodwin agreed to take charge of, and give every attention to, the fort, as soon as someone answered for its present state.[7]

These sudden inspections of the New Fort, and the questions being thrown at him about the condition of the buildings, made Thomas Scoble realize his tenancy at the New Fort may be coming to an end. He quickly shot off a telegram to Lieutenant-Colonel Wily, asking to be appointed caretaker of the New Fort, but it was of no use. On the evening of March 12, 1874, Goodwin instructed Scoble and the other residents of the fort to vacate the premises, by order of the minister of militia. Scoble immediately appealed again to Wily in Ottawa: "I beg that I may be informed whether this is at the instance of the Department of Militia and Defence; and if so if it is contemplated that I shall remove in this inclement season." He ended his letter with a gentle reminder about his earlier application for the position of caretaker of the New Fort. Scoble was promptly informed that his services as caretaker would not be required. However, the Department was willing to consider his request for continued occupancy of his quarters in the barracks, making it clear that Goodwin would be acting as caretaker, in charge of the property, and responsible for any repairs needed, and if Scoble were in fact allowed to remain, it would be strictly as a paying tenant, nothing more. The following month Scoble was informed that he would be allowed to stay at the New Fort, at an annual rental fee of $100, and a lease was prepared. Scoble happily accepted.[8]

STANLEY BARRACKS

THE NORTH-WEST MOUNTED POLICE

In the spring of that year, the garrison lands served once again as a concentration centre and training ground for recruits: this time, for Canada's new police force, the North-West Mounted Police. Prime Minister Sir John A. Macdonald, the man credited with the establishment of the N.W.M.P., first began planning the force in 1869, as part of the preparations for assuming control over the newly acquired Northwest Territory. The territory had been purchased in 1869 by the Dominion government from the Hudson's Bay fur trading company, which had formerly owned the land through British charter. Fears over Metis unease, Native hostility, and United States' schemes of annexation led the government to believe that it would be difficult to exert control over this vast area of land. A British Army officer, Lieutenant W.F. Butler of the 69th Regiment, was sent to survey the lands in question during 1870 and 1871 and prepare recommendations. His report concluded that law and order could be maintained by the establishment of a mobile, mounted force of 100 to 150 men under a civil magistrate or commissioner. In 1872, Ottawa sent Colonel Patrick Robertson-Ross, adjutant general of the Canadian militia, to carry out an additional reconnaissance of the Northwest Territory. Robertson-Ross reported back to Macdonald in December 1872 and recommended the organization of a regiment of 550 mounted riflemen, along with the establishment of a chain of military posts stretching from Manitoba to the Rockies.[9]

Macdonald himself envisioned the mounted police force as soldier-policemen: "It seems to me that the best Force would be, *Mounted Riflemen*, trained to act as cavalry, but also instructed in the Rifle exercises. They should also be instructed, as certain of the Line are, in the use of artillery, this body should not be expressly Military but should be styled *Police* and have the military bearing of the Irish Constabulary." The original name proposed for the force was the "North-West Mounted Rifles." When news of this appeared in the press, concern arose in Washington about Ottawa's actual intentions in creating this force. Consequently, Macdonald crossed out the word "Rifles" on the official draft and replaced it with the more civilian-sounding "Police."[10]

The Canadian Period (1870–1914)

Establishment of the force was delayed, however, because of the events unfolding at Red River in 1870. But in March 1873, Robertson-Ross's report became public, and this resulted in harsh criticism in the House of Commons of Macdonald's government and its failure to act on the report. The prime minister responded by announcing the government's intention to form a mounted police force for the northwest. Finally, in May 1873, a bill was passed authorizing the force, and on August 30, the force officially came into being through an Order-in-Council.[11] Again, events forced Ottawa to move quickly. In September, news broke of the Cypress Hills Massacre. A party of Assiniboine Natives had been slaughtered by a group of whites from Fort Benton, Montana. Over thirty men, women, and children were killed in the melee. Public outrage over this event, coupled with concern over the need to maintain law and order in the Northwest Territory, gave the government all the reason it needed to begin the creation of the mounted police force in earnest. On September 25, an Order-in-Council authorized the appointment of nine commissioned officers to the force. These nine immediately began recruiting the rest of the men who would fill the ranks of the N.W.M.P.[12]

At various centres in Ontario, including Toronto and Ottawa, as well as in Quebec and the Maritimes, the officers interviewed, tested, and signed up recruits. By October, three troops of fifty men had been raised. Lieutenant-Colonel George A. French, commander of "A" Battery, Royal Canadian Artillery, at Kingston, was appointed commissioner of the new force by Macdonald. At age thirty-two, French was a Royal Artillery captain who had been seconded to Canada with the acting rank of lieutenant-colonel while commanding Kingston's School of Gunnery.[13]

The uniform chosen for the force was a scarlet tunic, in imitation of that worn by the British regulars, and for a very practical reason. Robertson-Ross had noted in his report that:

> During my inspection in the North-West, I ascertained that some prejudice existed among the Indians against the colour of the uniform worn by the men of the Rifles, for many of the Indians said, "Who are those soldiers at Red River wearing dark clothes? Our old brothers who

formerly lived there (meaning H.M.S. 6th Regiment) wore red coats," adding, "we know that the soldiers of our great mother wear red coats and are our friends."[14]

In addition to the bright red tunic, the men of the N.W.M.P. wore dark cavalry riding breeches with two white stripes (later changed to scarlet stripes, and later changed again, this time to yellow); white helmets or forage caps; a leather belt with ammunition and revolver pouches on the sides; high black leather cavalry boots and spurs; white leather gauntlets; and a dark blue cavalry coat with a cape. Each constable was armed with a Snider carbine which, when on horseback, was carried in a carbine bucket at the side of the saddle.[15] New recruit William Parker looked forward to receiving and putting on his new uniform: "… it is very stylish," he wrote to his father; "the coat is scarlet & a very pretty shape & made for riding the pants are blue with white stripe down them top boots & spurs, cap with white round it."[16] Constables in the force received $1.00 per diem in pay, plus rations and uniforms. They signed three-year contracts, at the end of which they would receive a 160-acre (approximately one-quarter of a square mile) land grant in Manitoba or the Northwest Territory.[17]

Macdonald had planned to concentrate and train this first contingent of the N.W.M.P. at Toronto and Kingston during the winter of 1873–1874, before sending it west in the spring. However, fears of Native and Metis resistance, resulting largely from news of the Cypress Hill Massacre, prompted the government to send the recruits west before the close of navigation in 1873. These first 150 mounted police underwent their basic training at the "Stone Fort" — Fort Garry, Manitoba, during that winter, where they were organized into three fifty-man divisions, known as A, B, and C Troops. It was here, at Fort Garry, that the first 150 were officially sworn in as members of the North-West Mounted Police. The third recruit to take the oath was Sam Steele. Steele had been in Ottawa in August 1873 when he heard of the creation of the new mounted force. He hurriedly paid a visit to Colonel French, who also happened to be in Ottawa at the time, and obtained the colonel's permission to leave the artillery battery in order to join the N.W.M.P. Steele passed the required medical exam and was sworn into the force in September. On October 1, he assumed duties as sergeant-major of Division A, under Major Walsh.[18]

Because of the urgency of getting the first 150 recruits out west before winter set in, enlistment for this first contingent had turned into a mad rush. Applicants were not vetted as thoroughly as they should have been; some were found to be medically unfit, and many men who could barely ride, or who otherwise were unsuited for the job of mounted police constable, slipped through the application process. At the Stone Fort, it would be Sam Steele's job to attempt to teach them to ride.

Of the first 150, French dismissed two dozen on medical grounds, and nearly as many for misconduct. Clearly, reinforcements would be needed. In early February 1874, French returned to Ottawa to ask for more men for the force. He was rewarded with permission to increase the size of the force and authorization to purchase additional arms, ammunition, and supplies. French immediately set to work organizing three new divisions. He planned to accept more than 150 recruits this time, in order to compensate for the discharges and desertions that had taken place in A, B, and C Troops over the winter.[19]

This second round of N.W.M.P. recruiting began in the spring of 1874 in Toronto and Kingston. This time there was a huge pool of hopeful applicants to choose from. By now, word of the new force had spread and had captured the imagination of the Canadian public; hundreds of young men dreaming of adventure rushed to apply. The Toronto *Mail* reported that there were over 1,500 applicants. There were so many candidates, in fact, that Colonel French pleaded with the government to provide him with an assistant to help in handling the hundreds of applications: "'I am getting bushels of letters and telegrams and cannot answer or keep track of them.… From the time I arise in the morning until I go to bed at night I am working away.'"[20]

One morning in April 1874, a mathematics teacher in Montreal, Jean d'Artigue, was reading the Montreal *Witness* when the following ad caught his eye:

> The Dominion Government requires 150 volunteers
> for the North West Mounted Police. The knowledge of

English or French is obligatory. Moreover, the candidate must have good antecedents, and be a good horseman. For further particulars, apply to Colonel Bacon. — A. FRENCH, Commissioner.

D'Artigue had no idea of what a "mounted policeman" did, or even where the "North West" was; but he was definitely intrigued. He called on a friend, who patiently explained the nature of the new force and its mission. He also tried to discourage d'Artigue from applying. "My friend carefully pointed out the difficulties and dangers which this expedition would encounter, and said, in conclusion, that if everybody knew as much as he did about the North-West, the Government would not easily find 300 men who would thus run the risk of losing their scalps." D'Artigue carefully considered his friend's advice as he walked slowly back to his lodgings. But the reference to scalping, meant to scare him away from the prospect of enlisting, instead conjured up images in his mind of scenes from the novels of James Fenimore Cooper — stories that had so enthralled him as a boy. Now, here was his chance to experience that sort of adventure himself. D'Artigue applied, passed the medical exam, and was instructed to be at the Grand Trunk Railway station on April 16 to board a train for Toronto.[21]

D'Artigue headed home to pack. He also visited his friend to let him know that he had enlisted in the N.W.M.P. At first, his friend was incredulous. "One don't [sic] give up an advantageous career like yours, to embrace an adventurous one," he said, laughing. But once he realized how serious the young teacher was about his new profession, he did his best to try to talk him out of it. But d'Artigue would not be swayed. "I let him talk for an hour without interruption, and I am sure his reasons and arguments were good. But with my Quixotic ideas, and my young imagination of twenty years, I could only see fights, sieges, and victories."[22]

Because of the large pool of applicants for the second round of N.W.M.P. recruiting, Commissioner French could afford to be more selective. When recruiting was completed, he had a group of men who were healthier and more experienced than the previous year's batch. Many of the new recruits had been soldiers, and had strong military and riding experience. A total of two hundred had been chosen: 150 to form three new divisions, and 50 to supply reinforcements for the original three divisions. In April, the successful applicants were assembled at the New Fort in Toronto for training. Here, they were organized into divisions designated "D," "E," and "F." While the recruits began their crash course in drill, riding, and target practice, French, who arrived at the New Fort on April 21, was busy with administrative duties: ordering arms and clothing, arranging transportation, negotiating the purchase of pack animals and supplies.[23] One of the recruits at the New Fort, Fred Bagley, remarked that the commissioner "seemed to be here, there, and everywhere, giving special attention often accompanied by devastating remarks, to some of the incompetents wished on him by the Ottawa gang, and generally, a la Father O'Flynn, coaxing the lazy ones on 'wid a shtick.'"[24] French won the respect of many of the recruits by his remarkable ability to refer to them by name.[25]

In addition to the commissioner, several of the other officers of the force had military experience. The regimental sergeant-major in charge of drilling the recruits at the New Fort was Captain Tom Miles, formerly of the 13th Hussars; he was assisted by Sergeant Major Joe Francis, a Crimean War veteran who had taken part in the famous Charge of the Light Brigade as part of the 10th Light Dragoons. Artillery instruction was carried out by Inspector Jackson, an ex-officer from the battery at Kingston. Superintendent Carvell, assigned to command "E" Division, had served as an officer with the Confederate Army in the American Civil War; and, of course, out west there was Sergeant-Major Sam Steele, carrying out riding instruction at the Stone Fort. The presence of these men contributed to the development of a military-like structure and routine in the force.[26]

Of the three hundred men comprising the six divisions, 174 had previously performed some sort of military service: forty-one in the British regular service; eighty-seven in the Canadian militia; thirty-two in the Canadian Artillery ("A" and "B" Batteries); and fourteen in the Royal Irish Constabulary and Civil Police Forces. The force had a decidedly military nature in the first three decades of its existence. Regular drill instruction, military ceremonies, and the uniforms all reinforced the military image of the force, and also symbolized the social status attached to military activities, thus reinforcing the prestige of the force, and increasing its ability to command public support and co-operation.[27]

One significant difference between the N.W.M.P. and the military was that an effort was made in the N.W.M.P. not to recruit constables and non-commissioned officers from the lower end of the social hierarchy. Not only did the force promote an image of prestige and adventure, but recruitment took place in a period of economic depression, so the recruiters were able to be selective. The position of a N.W.M.P. officer was one of prestige and power. According to the recruitment records, the typical N.W.M.P. officer in the period 1873 to 1905 was Canadian-born, was drawn from the governing elite of eastern Canada, was either Anglican or Roman Catholic, frequently had a legal background, and almost certainly had some military experience and training. The elite nature of the force may be prescribed, perhaps, to the generally accepted beliefs of the time concerning the relationship between class and criminality: that crime was largely a lower-class phenomenon, and therefore law enforcement officers should be the social superiors of lawbreakers. In one of the first general orders issued by Commissioner French, he reminded sub-constables to consider themselves policemen, not militia, and to have the self-respect to refrain from committing the same offences as those whom they apprehended. French laid additional stress on the differences between a mounted police constable and a private soldier in the militia or regular forces by rejecting military punishments as degrading, and instituted fines and the threat of discharge in their place.[28]

Some of the recruits who trained at Toronto during April and May 1874 wrote vivid accounts of life in Toronto's New Fort. William Parker, who had enlisted as a sub-constable in 1874 at the age of twenty-one, wrote frequent letters home to his family in England, maintained diaries, and, after his retirement from the force in 1912, compiled reminiscences. Parker had left home in 1871, along with his brother Harry, because of the shortage of employment in England at that time. After some unsteady work as a farmhand in Ontario, and an unsuccessful search for land to lease, near the end of March 1874 he saw an advertisement for N.W.M.P. interviews taking place in London, Ontario. The twenty-one-year-old

The Canadian Period (1870–1914)

Eighteen-year-old William Parker, April 13, 1871, the year he immigrated to Canada from England in search of work. After three years of unsteady employment as a farmhand in Ontario, Parker responded to a North-West Mounted Police recruitment ad and was sent to Toronto's New Fort for training.

Glenbow Archives, NA-2235-1.

was enticed into applying by the good pay offered (seventy-five cents per day for sub-constables, and one dollar per day for constables), as well as by the fringe benefits: paid travelling expenses, "a bully good horse to ride upon," and the prospect of a grant of 160 acres of land after three years of service.[29]

Parker took the train from Sarnia to London, where Commissioner French planned to accept twelve recruits. On the appointed day, April 4, nearly two hundred hopeful applicants showed up at Tecumseh House to be interviewed by French. Selected by Commissioner French from the crowd of applicants, Parker passed the medical exam and was told to report to the New Fort in Toronto. Parker was delighted to have been accepted for the force. "Everybody around here thinks it is a splendid thing for a young man to go into," he wrote to his mother the next day.

Although there were rumours that the force would not last beyond the three-year enlistment period, Parker was not disheartened; if the force was disbanded, he would get his land grant all the same. "I shall also be able to save a good pile of money and if you come to look over the thing, it is a very good opening for me.… The colonel is a very nice man and if I behave myself properly I daresay he will push me on.…"[30]

Parker was sworn in as sub-constable on April 4, 1874, and arrived at the New Fort on April 10, where he was assigned to "D" Division. A few days later, he wrote his first letter home from the New Fort: "I arrived here last friday [*sic*] evening and like the life very well so far.…[We have] splendid rooms to sleep in, the size of rooms 40 x 30 twelve men in each, there are quite a lot of decent young fellows joined … I am very fond of drilling. In fact I was told that I had got on capitally, for one that had

Constable William Parker, North-West Mounted Police, Fort Macleod, Alberta, 1874. After nearly two months' training at the New Fort, Parker was officially a "Mountie." He thought his new uniform was "very stylish," according to a letter he wrote to his father.

Glenbow Archives, NA-2928-3.

never been drilled before." Despite a busy daily routine that began at half past six and consisted of cleaning and feeding of the horses, drill practice, and riding exercises, the recruits had free time from six until ten o'clock each evening, when they could visit the town; "so you see we have not bad times at all."[31]

Like the British regulars who had inhabited the barracks in years before, the mounted police recruits enjoyed pastimes such as game-hunting, cricket, and football, and also formed a band. On April 21, Parker wrote to his father: "… it is such a dreadful noisy place here that a fellow has not much chance to write a good letter. There are bagpipes being played right under me & the N.W.M.P. brass band is playing out side [*sic*] and four noisy fellows playing Euchre close beside me so I am pretty well surrounded."[32]

One of Parker's first tasks upon his arrival at the New Fort had been to fill his bed with straw. Another recruit found his accommodations even less favourable. Having travelled all night by train from Montreal, Jean d'Artigue arrived at the New Fort in the early hours of April 17, where he was shown into a large room containing only a table, and told that this would be his sleeping quarters. "I did not, for a moment, expect that this would be our sleeping quarters, until we were called out to get from the store a straw mattress and two blankets each. This looked very much like military life, and yet, we saw at the door an order, reminding us that we were not soldiers, but civilians."[33]

The youngest recruit was fifteen-year-old Fred Bagley. Bagley's father had served with Colonel French in the British Army, and when young Fred tried to enlist in the N.W.M.P., French immediately notified Bagley's father. After a heated confrontation, the father finally agreed to let his son enlist as a bugler, but only for a period of six months. Bagley was passed as "medically fit" and with the qualifying remark, "Very youthful but may develop." His family would not see him again for fourteen years.[34]

Like the teacher Jean d'Artigue, Bagley had been motivated by a quest for adventure:

> I had always been a close student of the works of James Fenimore Cooper, and imagined that life in the N.W.M.P.

would be one grand round of riding wild mustangs (I was always an expert horseman), chasing whisky traders and horse thieves, potting hostile savages, and hobnobbing with haughty Indian Princes and lovely unsophisticated Princesses. Alas! A few years in the service of the force sufficed to dissipate much of this glamour.

Some of the glamour must have been dissipated while still at the New Fort, where young Bagley was introduced to the duties of room orderly. In addition to his regular duties of attending drill and cleaning the barrack rooms and his duties as bugler, as room orderly Bagley also had to draw supplies for the cooks at "Ration Call," set the barrack room tables, bring the cooked food from the cookhouse, apportion it among the men, and, after the meal was over, wash the dishes and scrub the tables and benches. Aside from "an occasional 'kick' from a disgruntled trooper who thought I had not treated him fairly in the division of the spoil," the youngest recruit got along fairly well, even managing to escape being the victim of "the lighthearted practical jokes often played on the last joined recruit, such as sending him to the carpenter's shop to be 'measured for his sentry box'...."[35]

It is unclear which buildings of the New Fort were occupied by the force. The size of the barrack rooms as recorded by Parker, along with reports filed with the Department of Militia and Defence the following year regarding the condition of the barracks after their use by the N.W.M.P., indicate that one or both of the ranges of privates' barracks were used, and at least one room of the officers' quarters. Colonel Thomas Scoble, now leasing quarters for himself and his family at the New Fort, complained that the mounted police were using a lawn between the "rear of the buildings" and the lake as a ride, and destroying the grass; he appealed to the officer in command to prevent this destruction.[36]

The N.W.M.P. recruits occupied the New Fort until early June. In these two months they went through an intensive course of arms and foot drill, rifle practice, and artillery practice with the two nine-pounder field guns that had recently been brought over from England. Progress was good with many of the recruits having had previous experience in these skills. It was in the sessions of riding practice that, according to all accounts, chaos reigned. Although the recruiting ads for the force had specified that the candidates should be able to ride well, apparently many of them had overrated their abilities in this area. According to Parker, "the riding school was the most interesting, as the Sergt. Major standing in the centre of the circle with his long whip would drive us around bareback and when the command trot was given, quite a few would tumble off into the sawdust, then the Sergt. Major would shout out, 'Who told you to dismount.'" Fred Bagley also found the riding school quite comical: "A visit to the riding school revealed dashing horsemen galore. Many of them dashing from their saddles and over their horses [sic] heads...." He also referred to one particular recruit, "a former Professor in a famous French college" (Jean d'Artigue, no doubt), who "might be seen leaning forward from his saddle and embracing his horse's neck, drawing the raucous roar from the aforesaid R.R.S.M. [Rough Riding Sergeant-Major]: 'That's right young fellow me lad, kiss 'im and 'e'll be good to you.'"[37]

Jean d'Artigue, who had arrived at the New Fort from Montreal on April 17, joined the other recruits in foot drill the next day, and made good progress. A few days later, he began riding drill.

> I must say here, that most of us had overrated our proficiency in horsemanship; for when we came to ride without stirrups, many laughable falls ensued: men having lost their balance would cling to their horses in every imaginable position, till the drill-instructor coming up, would give the horse a smart lash with the whip, which would make him rear and plunge, till, freeing himself from his rider, he would gallop away to the stable. Even the officers were most of them as bad as ourselves at riding, but managed by some means, unknown to us, to get out of the *manège* drill, and went only to the field drill, where stirrups were allowed to be used. The Commissioner himself was a thoroughly well drilled officer; but most of the inspectors and sub-inspectors did not understand the simplest field manoeuvres; and

> their inefficiency was made manifest before we left Toronto.... Fortunately we had some of the sergeants from the regular army among us, who, on such occasions would come forward, put the officers in their proper places and restore us to order."[38]

Yet, by all reports, the horses at Toronto were the best available, and by the end of May the riding abilities of all the recruits had improved considerably.

After nearly two months at the New Fort, William Parker wrote in a letter to his father: "I still like the life very much; we live very well. I am very fat & strong; have played in two cricket matches since we have been here.... We are going to take up a lot of cricketing things with us [out west] so that we can still keep up the old game although we shall be a good way from our friends. The officers have bought two good footballs and we play some fiery old games of an evening. The horse that I have got now is an iron gray and he is a splendid fellow, can jump like a good bay...."[39]

During the time the recruits spent at Toronto, Commissioner French took the opportunity to try to shake the men of their James Fenimore Cooper–based visions of glory and adventure, and to warn the men about what lay ahead. Cecil Denny recalled many evenings spent in the mess room listening to French's descriptions of the land and the tasks that lay ahead. On two separate occasions, French assembled all ranks on parade and spoke bluntly about the hardships they would have to endure: camping on the open prairie; perhaps two or three days without food. He reminded the men that they were volunteers, and encouraged any man who felt he was not prepared for such a life to take his discharge now. A few did.[40]

On June 1, the recruits at the New Fort took the oath and were officially sworn in as members of the N.W.M.P. They spent the next three days carrying their gear to the Grand Trunk railway station. "On the fifth we had a holiday," reported d'Artigue. The following day, the men returned to the station with their horses, where they found "thousands of people" surrounding the station.[41]

After loading their horses into railway cars — no easy task — the men gathered in the dining room of the station for dinner. "Between the dinner and the departure, a music band played a good selection of a patriotic airs, reminding us of the services that the country expected from us. On every side, we were surrounded by an anxious crowd, each one wishing to shake hands with us once more. The hour of separation came at last. The train, which was to take one division and a half, was waiting. Final words were uttered …"[42] Young Fred Bagley's mother kissed him good-bye, and pressed a diary and a watch into his hands. "Be a good boy, say your prayers regularly and come back soon," she whispered.[43]

As the train pulled out of the station, most of the men were "in good spirits," reported d'Artigue — largely because of the amount of spirits they had imbibed during dinner. The train began to move; the band played "Auld Lang Syne," and the men sang "Vive la Canadienne" and "The Girl I Left Behind Me." The crowd waved and cheered. Less glamorous was the image of the few recruits who, fearful of Native scalping parties, had shaved their heads. The shorn heads protruding from the train windows prompted shouts of "Yoo-hoo, you jail birds!" as the trains departed.[44]

And so this force of sixteen officers, 201 men, and 244 horses, assembled and trained at the New Fort, departed Toronto. The train they were riding would take them through the United States, to Fargo, North Dakota — 1,300 miles, or more than 2,000 kilometres, away — the nearest point they could reach by train to Dufferin, Manitoba. From Fargo, they would march to Fort Dufferin to meet up with the first contingent, which was marching to Dufferin from the Stone Fort. "Toronto was soon behind us.…" remarked d'Artigue.[45]

THE INFANTRY SCHOOL

After the departure of the N.W.M.P. recruits, the New Fort was again, for the most part, unused and neglected during the next few years. However, suggestions to sell parts of the military reserve for development, or requests for lease of parts of the garrison buildings as quarters, continued to be rejected by the Department of Militia and Defence, with an eye to future military use of the land. The reserve, which originally measured approximately five hundred acres, had shrunken by this time to half that size, as a result of donations and sales of pieces for various purposes, and to various groups or individuals, or government branches, over the years. But with property values in Toronto rising, some believed that the military was losing a great opportunity to profit by not selling the land. William F. Coffin, the commissioner of ordnance and admiralty lands, suggested that the remaining 250 acres of military reserve lands be transferred to the Department of the Interior, divided up into "Villa Lots" and sold. Lieutenant-Colonel Powell, however, the acting adjutant general of militia and defence, protested to the minister. He pointed out that there was no other location for rifle practice available in or near Toronto. The retention of the military reserve lands, he argued, did not interfere in any way with the progress of the city of Toronto, as there was an abundance of land in other directions for the city to expand. The temporary leasing of areas of land not immediately required by the military was reasonable, he argued, but not their "alienation by sale."[46]

In March 1875, Major-General Edward Selby-Smyth, general officer commanding the Canadian militia, visited the New Fort in order to report back to the minister of militia and defence on its condition. He arrived in the middle of a blizzard. Wading through deep drifts of snow, the general made his way to the privates' barracks and the officers' quarters, and was shocked by what he found. "I was struck with the neglected and dirty state in which I found [the New Fort]," he wrote in his report. "It appears that when the Mounted Police were en route for Manitoba they were permitted to inhabit these barracks and on quitting them the rooms were left uncleaned and the rubbish and dirt still remains. Several of the Stoves are perishing from rust." He found numerous broken window fastenings and broken window panes, through which significant amounts of snow were blowing into the buildings. "One room in the Officers' Quarters has been used either as a dog kennel, or for some sort of wild beasts — it was filthy and the floor littered with dirty straw and excrement. These Barracks are costly buildings — well worth preserving by repair." Selby-Smyth at once authorized the storekeeper, Goodwin, to employ a fatigue party of the "A" Battery of Artillery to nail up the windows and to commence the clean-up and repairs. But he also expressed some concerns about the storekeeper. Goodwin, he noted in his report, was "a very worthy and excellent old man — full of good intentions," but was now nearly ninety years of age and incapable of fulfilling the duties of storekeeper. Selby-Smyth recommended that Goodwin be allowed to retire, and provided with a pension, "as a Reward for a long Career distinguished by integrity."[47] A few military families occupying premises at the New Fort were allowed to remain as tenants, but the Department of Militia and Defence remained reluctant to sell any land that might be needed for military purposes, or to allow any use of the reserve that might interfere with the use of the rifle range. Meanwhile, the city of Toronto continued to expand and conflicts inevitably arose between the City and the Department over the use of the Common.

By 1878, Toronto City Council had recognized the value of the Agricultural Exhibition to the city. Realizing that the current Exhibition grounds, just south of the Crystal Palace, were no longer large enough for the needs of a full-fledged fair, in March the City negotiated with the military to lease the westerly portion of the garrison reserve (close to fifty-two acres, or twenty-one hectares) for a term of twenty-one years, renewable, at $100 per year, as Exhibition grounds. This plot of land included 450 feet (close to 137 metres) of lake frontage, and is part of today's C.N.E. grounds. Several permanent exhibition buildings were built, and the Crystal Palace was dismantled and moved to the new grounds. These developments helped Toronto to secure the 1878 provincial fair; but in 1879, the fair moved to Ottawa, and Toronto formed the Industrial Exhibition Association, in order to stage its own annual fair, to be held each September. Not surprisingly, after years of resistance to doling out parts of the military reserve, this development surprised and concerned many of the other users of the military reserve. Lieutenant-Colonel William D. Otter, secretary of the Ontario Rifle Association, sent a statement from the Association to the minister of militia and defence, stating unequivocally that the use of part of Garrison Common for exhibition purposes would interfere with the Association's annual

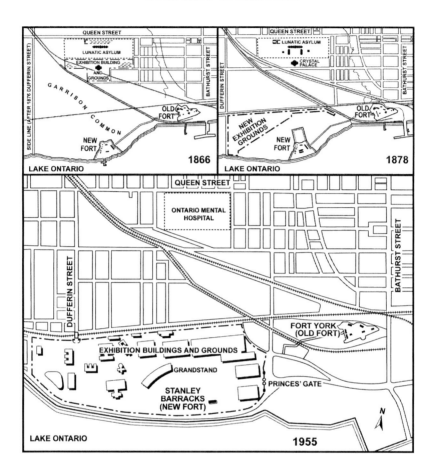

Over the years, the military reserve shrank drastically in size, as the City of Toronto and the Exhibition grounds expanded.

Compiled by Karen Hansen, Hansen Designs, based on maps in the collection of the Toronto Public Library (TPL), specifically: "City of Toronto, Compiled from Surveys made to the present date, 1866"; "Map of Toronto, Published by Miles & Co., Drawn by A.T. Cotterell, C.E., Revised to April 1st, 1878"; and "The Toronto Harbour Commissioners Condition Plan, 1st January 1955."

matches, as well as with the regular practice of the Active Militia. As a result, the continued existence of the Rifle Association was now in question, and needlessly so, since land for the exhibition could have easily been found elsewhere.[48]

There was certainly some justification to Otter's claims. Rifle practice on the Common had to be discontinued during the annual exhibition.

The Canadian Period (1870–1914)

And there were additional complications, more headaches for the military. The Exhibition Association asked that it be allowed to install a temporary gate through the fence on Garrison Common, in order to allow exhibition visitors to get from the Exhibition grounds to see the military review at the New Fort in September 1879. This was allowed, but resulted in further infringement on the military's land. Military authorities complained that the "Opening made by Exhibition people leads directly on our parade could never keep the ground if left open — recommend it be shut up."[49]

And demands on the military for use of its land did not let up. Finally, in 1880, when the Toronto Cricket Club asked to lease part of Garrison Common as a cricket ground, Major-General Selby-Smyth expressed the military's frustration:

> The loss of the ground already given to the Exhibition Society has greatly cramped the Common for Military purposes — on the ocasion [sic] of the Review last September I required double the amount of room for the troops on the ground — I think it unfair that every body of persons who wants a bit of ground for their use, thinks that military ground is the first they may hope to obtain, because it is not in use for Military Service every day in the year.[50]

The Ontario Rifle Association tried to hold its ground. In November, it leased approximately 114 acres of Garrison Common land, for a period of ten years (renewable), at $40 per year. Late the following year, Otter requested permission to move into one of the buildings of the New Fort for the upcoming summer months. Since he would need to be on hand constantly at the rifle ranges to supervise improvements and alterations that needed to be made to the ranges, having quarters nearby would facilitate his work. The request was approved, and a lease prepared for Otter in February 1882.[51]

In 1883, the long-anticipated new military use for the Common and the New Fort materialized with the revival of the militia schools

STANLEY BARRACKS

"*Toronto — The New Fort: the Gray Battery Under Inspection; Officers' Quarters, Laboratory, &c., in rear,*" 1876. Downtown Toronto can be seen in the background in the upper image.

_{Canadian Illustrated News, Vol. XIV, No. 10, September 16, 1876, p. 145, Library and Archives Canada, C-064560.}

of the 1860s. The schools had lapsed as a result of the departure of the British regulars from Canada. The Canadian government's attempt to reinstate militia schools in each of the military districts that had been established across the country had failed. By 1874, these district schools had closed, suffering from a lack of equipment and qualified instructors. British officers still in Canada urged the Canadian government to establish a Permanent Force to serve as a training cadre for the militia. Finally, in the early summer of 1883, Minister of Militia Adolphe Caron put before cabinet a proposal to create infantry and cavalry schools at Toronto, Montreal, and Fredericton. These schools would constitute an officer education system, based on the 1860s model. All militia officers would be required to attend the appropriate school to qualify for their appointments. Accordingly, a new Militia Act was passed that year authorizing the establishment (in addition to the Active Militia force) of one troop of cavalry, a third battery of artillery, and three companies of infantry, to total no more than 750 men. These corps were to perform garrison duties, including aid to the civil power, as well as serve as schools of instruction for the officers and other ranks of the militia.[52] The three artillery batteries were brigaded as the Regiment of Canadian Artillery (RCA); the Cavalry and Infantry School Corps would develop into the Royal Canadian Dragoons and the Royal Canadian Regiment. A Canadian Permanent Force had been established, and it was stepping into the role that the British garrisons in Canada had played until 1870.

Almost immediately, Lieutenant-Colonel Otter wrote to Caron, asking for an appointment in the new corps. In late July he received the reply: he had been appointed commandant of one of the infantry schools. The three infantry school companies were to be located in abandoned British barracks at Fredericton, Saint Jean (Quebec), and Toronto. Otter was assigned to command "C" Company, which would be housed in Toronto's New Fort. Otter would receive $4.00 per day pay, plus $1.25 command pay, as well as fuel, light, barrack accommodation, and forage for a horse. The buildings of the New Fort required some immediate repairs; in the meantime, recruiting was begun for one hundred men to complete "C" Company. In November, the Toronto *Globe* reported that repairs were well underway, and that Otter's residence would be habitable by the first week of December.[53]

Toronto's infantry school opened on April 1, 1884. A few days later, a *Globe* reporter visited the new school and found that the New Fort had sprung to life once again. "In the fort matters certainly look 'military,'" he wrote, "and put one in mind of the old days when hussars and artillerymen filled the parade ground and drank each other's health at the same canteen." The reporter was also impressed by the condition of the barracks:

> The quarters of … the non commissioned officers and men, are very comfortably fitted up, and ablution, bath rooms, *etc* are now being added, supplied with hot and cold water. There are now some eight large rooms fitted up for their use, each one containing twelve single beds, which are folded up every morning and remain in that

STANLEY BARRACKS

The Guard Room, New Fort, Toronto, 1887.

William Dillon Otter Collection, Library and Archives Canada, C-031393.

The canteen at the New Fort Barracks, Toronto, 1887. According to The Guide, *a manual for the Canadian militia authored by Otter in 1880, "Canteens, where established in quarters, are for the exclusive use and accommodation of the troops, and for the ready supply to the soldiers of such liquors or other provisions as could not be easily procured otherwise...." The only beverages sold at the infantry school's canteen were beer and ginger ale; profits were used to buy boats for the men's rowing club. (See Morton,* The Canadian General, *92.)*

William Otter Collection, Library and Archives Canada, C-031462.

position till night to prevent the men from lounging when off duty. The hospital is fitted up with two wards, one of which is set apart for contagious diseases.... The canteen looks like a neat grocery store with its beer tap in the corner, where the married men's families have their wants supplied, and where the men can have their beer although it must not be drunk there, but in a room across the hall fitted up for the purpose.

A recreation room above the canteen contained a bagatelle and billiard table; there was also a reading room for the men.[54]

According to the same reporter, the officers' quarters were also "handsomely fitted up." Colonel Otter's quarters consisted of four large rooms and a bath on the second storey. Also on this floor were captain's quarters, rooms for several other officers, and a storeroom and billiard room. The first (ground) floor contained a mess room, with anteroom and pantry across the hall; additional officers' quarters; offices; and four more rooms for the use of the commandant and captain. The basement contained the kitchen, larder, wine cellar, storerooms, and quarters for the cook, mess butler, and other servants. There were also separate kitchens for the commandant and captain, and for their servants.[55]

The original barrack master's stores building (next to the canteen, on the west side of the fort) was now to be used as a hospital. The original hospital building, located on the north side of the square, opposite the officers' quarters, had been converted for use as orderly room, brigade office and quarter master's stores. Its upper storey, meanwhile, would serve as married officers' quarters, and quarters for Lieutenant-Colonel Alger, superintendent of stores. A number of small frame cottages, grouped together in the fort's southwest corner, provided quarters for the nine married men in the corps and their families.[56]

The main shortcoming of the militia schools of the 1860s, according to Otter, had been the fact that militia officers only attended for a few hours each day. In contrast, when the infantry schools were established in 1884, the attendees ate their meals at the school, slept at the school, and were engulfed in the military atmosphere at all times — thus

STANLEY BARRACKS

The sergeants' mess, New Fort Barracks, Toronto, 1887.

William Dillon Otter Collection, Library and Archives Canada, C-031458.

The officers' mess room, 1894. All officers were required to belong to the mess, and each week a committee was detailed to direct the mess and ensure that all mess rules were carried out.

William Dillon Otter Collection, Library and Archives Canada, C-031435.

providing a better, more complete, military education. Otter was also delighted to have Sergeant-Major Fred Gathercole as drill instructor at the school. Gathercole had been drill instructor in the 16th Imperials. Otter knew he was good; he had been Otter's own drill instructor when Otter had taken his officers' course in the early 1860s.[57]

The Toronto school was successful in its first year. According to a report filed by Otter on December 27, 1884, of thirty-nine officers enrolled in the school, twenty-seven had obtained certificates; only ten had withdrawn, or failed to pass; two were still in the school. Of fifty-six non-commissioned officers and men, twenty-five had obtained certificates; fourteen had been dismissed, or failed to pass, while seventeen remained in the school. Major-General Frederick D. Middleton, newly appointed as the general officer commanding of the Canadian militia, visited the school in July of 1884 and praised its progress. Much of the credit for the success of the New Fort school went to Otter, who not only served as an example of an accomplished military man to the young officers, but, through his administrative skills and painstaking attention to detail, by all accounts ran the school like an efficient business.[58]

The gymnasium at the New Fort, 1887.

William Dillon Otter Collection, Library and Archives Canada, C-031442.

STANLEY BARRACKS

Despite the repairs to the New Fort that had been hastily completed in 1883 to accommodate the opening of the infantry school, its residents were not finding the barracks to be very comfortable as living quarters. Gilbert Elliot had found the officers' quarters frightfully cold when he was stationed at the New Fort in the 1840s, and it seemed to those residing in the same building forty years later that things had not much improved. Otter repeatedly appealed for central heating for the officers' quarters, and for a more modern system of lighting to replace coal oil. When these requests were refused, his wife, Molly, took it upon herself to write directly to the minister of militia, suggesting that long-overdue repairs to the other ranks' quarters be postponed, in order that the commandant's quarters might have a furnace. "Life is so short," she wrote in her letter to Caron, "… that it seems very dreadful for six months of the year to be made unhappy because one can't keep oneself warm."[59]

And there were more serious problems. The surgeon of the Infantry School reported to Colonel Otter in the summer of 1892 that the earth closet latrines that were attached to the married sergeants' and men's quarters were posing a serious health hazard, and needed to be moved several feet away from the buildings. The action was approved, but for some reason delayed, until in December when the colour sergeant of No. 2 Company, who resided in one of the affected buildings, suffered an attack of typhoid fever. Otter was convinced the disease was contracted through the proximity of the latrines to the living quarters. There were also concerns that unsanitary latrine conditions could spark another cholera epidemic; there had been several such epidemics in Canada in the nineteenth century. Late that month, a local contractor was finally hired to carry out the necessary work.[60]

Aside from the physical condition of the buildings, the new schools faced other challenges. It was sometimes hard to find the best recruits, because the pay offered was at British rates, although the cost of living was higher in Canada. By the 1890s, Canadian pay rates were lower than British rates, N.W.M.P. rates, and United States Army rates. There was still no pension for service in the Permanent Force, and opportunities for advancement were few.[61] Consequently, there were few inducements to join, and desertion further lessened the strength of the corps. There was

The Canadian Period (1870–1914)

A lawn tennis party being held on the grounds of the New Fort in 1890. A section of the officers' quarters is visible in the extreme right side of the photo.

William Dillon Otter Collection, Library and Archives Canada, C-031363.

also the hostility of many Canadians toward the Permanent Force. Even with the withdrawal of British forces from Canada, many Canadians had opposed the creation of a standing army, resenting the financial outlay, and holding to the traditional view that the militia was the true, and best, defender of Canada. Meanwhile, the militia feared that the existence of a permanent corps would not only usurp their role, but would result in decreased financial appropriations for the militia. In defence of the Permanent Force, the government stressed the instructional, rather than the combat, role of the corps.[62]

A Toronto author, writing under the pen name of "Dom Pedro," aptly expressed the apprehension shared by many Canadians towards the regular army as he described the New Fort in 1891:

> The waves still lap against the masonry shore. The guns still menace the invader. The bullets still fly at large on the Garrison Common. The quadrangular buildings

of the New Fort have not deviated one quarter of an inch from their foundations since they were first built. But a change has taken place in the internal arrangement of the New Fort. All the high carnival sort of fun has departed with the volunteer troops. Everything is now orderly, regular and ominous of serious discipline. Every man is a machine, that acts with perfect accuracy, when the operator touches a button.[63]

Toronto's interest in the corps had been revived somewhat in 1885, when five officers and eighty-five men of "C" Company from the New Fort, accompanied by 250 volunteers, were sent to put down the North-West Rebellion. Divided into two sections, "C" Company took part in three of the principal engagements of the campaign. Upon the troops' return to Toronto, a huge congratulatory crowd, led by the mayor, greeted them at the train station. From there, the soldiers marched along King Street and back the New Fort. A banquet was held that night for the men of "C" Company, and the following evening, a mess dinner for Otter and his officers. As a further tribute, an illuminated address, signed by 586 Torontonians, was presented to Otter, expressing admiration and appreciation for his contributions to the city, and to the nation, as a member of the Queen's Own Rifles, as commandant of the Infantry School, and as secretary of the Ontario Rifle Association.[64]

However, relations between the military and the civilian populations of Toronto were far from smooth. In 1891, for example, the Toronto Orchestral Association protested to Otter and then over his head directly to Caron that the bandsmen of "C" Company, Infantry School Corps, stationed at the New Fort, were coming into the city, changing into civilian clothes, and hiring themselves out for musical engagements in the city at low rates, thereby creating unfair competition for the musicians of Toronto. Military officials, finding no contravention of Militia Orders in this situation, refused to take action to stop the "C" Company bandsmen.[65]

A more serious matter arose over the use of the rifle range. As secretary of the Ontario Rifle Association, Otter had been embroiled for several years in the conflict over encroachment by the City, and, in particular,

The Canadian Period (1870–1914)

by the Exhibition, onto the military reserve. The rifle range, located on the shoreline west of the New Fort, was an issue of particular controversy, because of the danger it posed as civilian usage of the Garrison Common area increased. Toronto writer "Dom Pedro" described the problem from the viewpoint of Toronto's civilian population:

> The trouble is, the soldiers do not discriminate between a friend and an enemy. Such bullets that do not hit the targets, or get buried in the mounds behind the targets, rake the lake shore beyond, and often find lodgement in persons who knowingly or unknowingly place themselves in line with the ranges, perhaps in the pursuit of pleasure or a stroll on the wharf for a little fresh air, or perhaps taking the shortest way home by boat. These very ignorant persons do not know what resistance the atmosphere offers to the force of a leaden bullet from a Martini rifle at five hundred yards.[66]

The issue came to a head in the summer of 1887, when Perley Macdonald, the eldest son of the managing director of the Confederate Life Insurance Company, was struck by a bullet from a Snider-Enfield while rowing in a small boat on the lake near the range, where two or three corps of the Active Militia were practising. Macdonald died the next day. A court of inquiry was assembled at the New Fort to investigate, comprised of a three-member board presided over by Colonel Casimir Gzowski, and the deputy adjutant generals of Military Districts No. 1 and No. 2, Lieutenant-Colonel Jackson and Lieutenant-Colonel Otter. Over the course of the next three days, the board examined witnesses, and released its findings on September 16. The board concluded that the deadly bullet almost certainly did come from the range, but that the range had taken the normal and required precautions, including flying danger flags on the target butts — that is, the "stop butts" that were placed behind the targets to stop stray bullets. The board also made a point of stressing that this was only the second such accident in the twenty years that the Garrison Common range had been in use, a period during which, it was estimated, "upwards of one million rounds of ball ammunition" had been fired; and, as no more suitable or safer range could be procured within a reasonable distance of the city, closing the range would inconvenience and damage the efficiency of the local militia. The board's recommendation was that the stop butts be raised and extended, or that a line of buoys be placed in the water to mark the limits of safety for boats on the lake.[67]

Still, the controversy continued. Torontonians were not as convinced as Otter wanted them to be that the ranges were safe. Boat owners complained that their vessels and sails often had been struck with bullets as they sailed past the range, and that they feared bodily injury to themselves. More than two dozen businessmen involved in the shipping of stone across the lake wrote a joint letter to Minister of Militia Caron, insisting that the rifle range was hurting their business. Several of their vessels had been hit by bullets from the range, they claimed, and they had the marks on the hulls and sails to prove it.[68]

One Torontonian's sarcastic description of the situation, while meant to be humorous, was probably not too far off the mark in reflecting the sentiment of many of the residents of the city at the time: that the military was demonstrating a shameful lack of regard for the safety of Toronto's civilian population. It was the duty of military authorities, he wrote:

> [T]o point out to those persons, who do not know any better than to live in the west end of the city, that it would be more comfortable if they wore armour without any joints in it while passing in front of the Butts, and at the same time the steamboat companies might build a new line of steamers, completely iron-clad with no port holes, and have the decks cleared when rounding for Dufferin Street wharf. Of course this comes expensive, and the population in that part of the city is increasing, but the militia can't help that; a fair warning is a fair warning. It only remains for the citizens who are compelled to use the lake front up there to be very

careful and dodge the bullets, and recommend to the military people to put white feathers on their bullets to facilitate the dodging. For it is certain the bullets will not dodge the citizens.… It is a choice whether the butts or the city should be removed. It is the duty of all peaceable citizens to find a new site for the city."[69]

The year after the Perley Macdonald incident, another charge of alleged carelessness in target practice was levelled against the military, after a Torontonian's account of a close call while out on the lake was published in the Toronto *Empire* in June 1888. L.H. Baldwin described sailing near Jameson Avenue near the New Fort. As the wind dropped, he began to row, and it being after 6:30 p.m., he assumed any target practice would have ended for the day and it was safe to row close to shore. Upon hearing rifle shots, he decided that hugging the shore as closely as possible was the safest bet — "so that any stray bullets go over me." But he had to row farther from the shore in order to get around the Exhibition Wharf, and as he did, a stray bullet passed over his head. He reported to Otter that no buoys were in place to warn of the danger. Otter ordered the ranges closed until he could investigate the matter. In the meantime, a number of members of the Queen's Own Rifles and the Royal Grenadiers signed a resolution stating that if target practice were permanently suspended, they would quit the force. By the end of the month, Otter had submitted his findings to Ottawa. Despite Baldwin's claims to the contrary, Otter insisted that all proper precautions had been taken and warnings given. He warned of the detrimental effect that the closing of the ranges would have on annual target practice and the efficiency of the local corps. Eventually, the problem was solved, once and for all, when Otter was able to arrange for the transfer of the ranges to Mimico, at municipal expense.[70]

Despite such conflicts as the one over the safety of the rifle ranges, when the military considered the removal of troops from Toronto, Torontonians displayed a fierce loyalty to the local corps. In 1897, when news broke that a squadron of Dragoons stationed at the New Fort was going to be withdrawn, Mayor John Shaw wrote to the minister of militia in protest, calling it a gross injustice to a city of the size and importance of Toronto.[71]

STANLEY BARRACKS

THE PERMANENT FORCE

The Infantry School Corps functioned as three distinct companies, united on paper and by similarity of uniform, equipment, and duties. However, in such a scattered system, it was hard to achieve any sense of regimental unity or *esprit de corps*, and this too was detrimental to the corps. In 1892, the general officer commanding, Major-General I.J.C. Herbert, decided to improve the morale and efficiency of the permanent corps by adopting a regimental system. The four companies of infantry[72] were united under the name of the "Canadian Regiment of Infantry." The following year, the regiment received a royal prefix and permission to wear the imperial cipher, V.R.I. — *Victoria Regina Imperatrix*.[73] The cavalry school at Quebec was amalgamated with the Mounted Infantry School that had been established in 1885 at Winnipeg to form a regiment known as the "Canadian Dragoons" (later the "Royal Canadian Dragoons"), with troops at Toronto and Winnipeg. At the same time, the Regiment of Canadian Artillery was re-organized and enlarged. Through these changes, Herbert hoped to create a more uniform, practical, and sound system of instruction, and to turn the schools into not just places of elementary military instruction, but "centres of military thought," as well.[74]

The year 1893 was marked by two major events. The New Fort was given the official name of "Stanley Barracks," in honour of Frederick Arthur Stanley, Lord Stanley of Preston, governor general of Canada from 1888 to 1893, as he prepared to return to England.[75] This was also the year that the Royal Canadian Dragoons moved to Toronto. From the very beginnings of the Permanent Force, there had been steady, ongoing pressure to move the cavalry school from Quebec to Ottawa, Kingston, or Toronto. Of the 1,944 militia cavalrymen in the Dominion, 1,017 were in Ontario. On August 21, 1893, the Dragoons shifted base to Stanley Barracks.[76]

In May 1898, the permanent corps was once again called into action. A Yukon Field Force was being raised to assist the Mounted Police in the supervision of the Yukon gold rush area. Any one of the three Permanent Force units would have been unable to provide enough men for the Field Force, given their numerous other tasks related to the training of the Active Militia. Therefore, the various units were all ordered to provide

The Canadian Period (1870–1914)

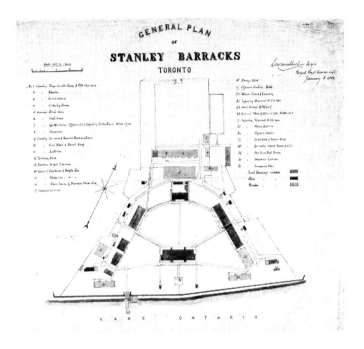

A plan of the New Fort, now called Stanley Barracks, in 1894. A visitor described the layout of the fort: "Its buildings forming a quadrangle and surrounded by a high board fence; the whole occupying about eight acres of good arable land.... In the centre of the quadrangle is a square block of green sward, neat and trim, with a gravelled roadway, forming on its outer sides. The two-storey stone building on the north of the green patch is the quarters of the Commandant, and office. The building is quite modern, gothic in architecture, with balcony in front. Directly opposite, at the south of the square, is a stone building, three times as long, plain, high steps leading into it, like the arches of a Chinese bridge, and crowned with a slate roof. Seeing orderlies passing to and from the Commandant's residence, it follows this must be the quarters of the general officers. The east and west sides of the square are flanked by long two storied buildings, similar to the last mentioned, only twice as long. The east building is devoted to the departments of kitchen, sergeants' mess, armory, storehouse, etc. The west twin for the canteen, the quarters of the privates, etc." (Dom Pedro, "Old Times at the New Fort," 1891, 9–10.)

Lawrence Buchan, "General Plan of Stanley Barracks, Toronto," [1894], Library and Archives Canada, NMC 23160.

STANLEY BARRACKS

Infantry School Commandant William D. Otter and his men at the main gate of Stanley Barracks, 1894. The east gate was the main entrance to the New Fort. A visitor in 1891 described this entranceway: "If the visitor should wish to penetrate the interior of Toronto's great protector, he would have to consult the sentry who marches to and from the high posted gateway through the building, and the archway, some thirty feet distant, dressed in the uniform of the School of Infantry, red striped trousers, red coat and Scotch cap, well whitened belts, all denoting neatness and order, pacing with short quick steps, and rifle at the trail. If the aforesaid sentry thought you merited his august permission, the visitor could at once go through the archway and pass the rack containing long and short rifles, on the right wall, bearing in mind, though, to walk with a strictly military gait. After passing through the archway, the mysteries of the New Fort would unfold before him." (Dom Pedro, "Old Times at the New Fort," 1891, 9–10.)

William Dillon Otter Collection, Library and Archives Canada, C-031375.

The Canadian Period (1870–1914)

Company mess room, Royal Canadian Regiment, 1894.

William Dillon Otter Collection, Library and Archives Canada, C-031348.

men. The completed Field Force, which included a detachment from Toronto, consisted of sixteen officers and two hundred other ranks. Among these were sixteen Royal Canadian Dragoons and 133 men of the Royal Canadian Regiment. In the Yukon, the Field Force undertook normal garrison duties, as well as police and customs duties.[77]

The Royal Canadian Dragoons and Royal Canadian Regiment at Stanley Barracks also served in South Africa, after war erupted between Britain and the two Boer republics, Transvaal and the Orange Free State. Britain requested assistance from Canada and other members of the British Commonwealth. In October of 1899, the 2nd (Special Service) Battalion, RCR, was raised, consisting of eight companies of infantry (of 125 men each). These companies were designated "A" through "H." "C" Company was recruited in Toronto.[78] The battalion was recruited largely from the Active Militia, but included a cadre of regulars and was commanded by a Canadian Permanent Force officer, Colonel Otter. Otter's wife, Molly, remained in residence at the Stanley Barracks officers' quarters while her husband was serving in South Africa.[79]

Britain soon asked for a second contingent for the South African campaign, but stipulated that it should include cavalry and artillery detachments of trained men. Consequently, the Royal Canadian Dragoons were expanded to two battalions, each with two squadrons of 371 all ranks and 275 horses. Each squadron consisted of four troops. The first battalion, recruited in the eastern provinces and Manitoba, was made up of officers and men of the Royal Canadian Dragoons and militia cavalrymen; the other battalion was raised in the northwest, and was formed around a cadre of N.W.M.P. The battalions were named 1st and 2nd Battalions, Canadian Mounted Rifles.[80]

"A" Squadron of the 1st Battalion was recruited in Ontario and western Quebec. Toronto served as the concentration centre for "A" Squadron's first troop (recruited in Toronto), second troop (recruited in Toronto and St. Catharines), and fourth troop (raised in London and Kingston). Training and preparation took place at the various regimental concentration centres. The daily routine consisted of three to four hours of drill, lessons in the theory of mounted infantry tactics, caring for the horses, fitting of uniforms and equipment, and drawing of supplies. The only free time remaining for the men was after church parade on Sundays.[81] The Canadian Mounted Rifles, along with three batteries of artillery, reached South Africa in March of 1900. Among those who left from Stanley Barracks was Lieutenant-Colonel E. Arthur Steer, who had enlisted in the Royal Canadian Dragoons in Winnipeg in 1897. Steer had served in the Yukon Field Force, as one of the sixteen Dragoons assigned to assist the N.W.M.P. to maintain law and order in the Klondike, and afterwards was stationed at Stanley Barracks. From there, he was shipped to South Africa.[82]

Bugler Daniel Stevens was so anxious to see action in South Africa that he departed from Stanley Barracks without leave, joining Lord Strathcona's Horse at Halifax as they embarked. Colonel Otter, who had been cabled about Stevens's adventure, wired Stevens instructions to proceed to the front, where he was made senior bugler. After nine months' service, Stevens returned to Toronto.[83]

The Canadian Period (1870–1914)

Stevens's case was not unique. Men of the Permanent Force, who were still being paid the 1883 wage of forty cents per day, generally were eager to serve in South Africa, where the men of the Canadian Mounted Rifles received seventy-five cents per day. Some men even dropped their commissions to enrol as privates. On the home front, the regulars' duties were monotonous in comparison, and the number of desertions increased. In 1901, among 167 men of the Royal Canadian Dragoons and the Royal Canadian Regiment at Stanley Barracks, 46 deserted.[84]

After the Canadian Mounted Rifles departed for South Africa, it was discovered that some of them left their barracks rooms in the New Fort in an utter mess. Three rooms, which had been occupied by the non-commissioned officers and men of the 1st and 2nd troops of "A" Squadron, were left filthy with dirt, and strewn with broken stove pipes, smashed coal scuttles, and broken dishes and bottles all over the floor. Although the men responsible had already sailed for South Africa, the matter was taken very seriously by authorities, who decided to issue a reprimand to the men, as well as to charge them for the damages through stoppages in their pay.[85]

In October 1899, a more serious scandal involving troops at Stanley Barracks erupted when a Toronto newspaper reported that a Member of Parliament, Joseph-Israël Tarte, had been burned in effigy at Stanley Barracks, while soldiers gleefully danced around. (Tarte, who was serving as minister of public works in Prime Minister Wilfrid Laurier's cabinet, was a controversial figure who had been very outspoken in his opposition to the participation of Canadian troops in the South African War.) Otter demanded an explanation from Lieutenant-Colonel Lessard, commanding officer of the RCD at Stanley Barracks. After investigating, Lessard reported to Otter that a few men at the barracks had been playing with an old Victoria Cross dummy, kicking it about, when someone set fire to it. While it was burning, one of the men, a Private Coggins, shouted the name of the Honourable Mr. Tarte. Coggins, who had been with the squadron for two years and was generally of good character, was drunk and irresponsible at the time of this unfortunate incident, explained Lessard. He had been punished, and he had apologized. Lessard hurried to assure Otter that the dummy had in no way been intended to represent

Tarte, nor had the men danced around the burning figure. Otter was satisfied with Lessard's explanation and his handling of the matter.[86]

Toronto's martial spirit received a major boost in October 1901, when the Duke and Duchess of Cornwall and York paid a royal visit to the city. Garrison Common sprang to life as a colossal military review took place on October 11. Eleven thousand militia troops had been mustered for the event, and they were quartered in tents and buildings on the Exhibition grounds. This encampment became known as "Exhibition Park Camp."[87]

Toronto's permanent troops returned to Stanley Barracks after the war, and resumed their role of training the militia. It was at this time that the Dragoons became famous for their Musical Ride. The first cavalry version of the ride had been performed in North America at the 1893 Chicago World's Fair, by a party of ex-British cavalrymen. Several of these horsemen came to Canada and enlisted in the Royal Canadian Dragoons. One of them established a Dragoon Musical Ride, which was first performed in 1894 in Toronto. The Ride, or "drill pattern formation riding to music at three and a bit paces," consisted of the paces of walk, trot, and canter, and ended with a final cavalry charge towards the audience, with an abrupt, last-minute halt. (This final gallop was not far enough to be called a pace.) The riding team consisted of forty men and horses (thirty-two to perform, eight as spares). The riders wore their dress uniforms, consisting of blue pantaloons, red tunics, white cross belts and gloves, and brass helmets with black plumes; they carried lances with fluttering pennons. The Ride proved to be an extremely popular attraction at exhibitions and horse shows around the world until the Second World War, when the regiment's conversion to armour brought an end to the event. It was continued, however, by the Mounted Police, who had been taught the manoeuvres by the Royal Canadian Dragoons, and is now performed by the R.C.M.P. in their public appearances across the nation.[88]

Ironically, while the Dragoons' Musical Ride was an immensely popular feature of the Exhibition grandstand show each fall, the success of the Exhibition (by now known as the Canadian National Exhibition, or C.N.E.) was beginning to threaten the Dragoons' facilities at Stanley Barracks, through its continuous encroachment on the garrison lands. Toronto City Council regarded the success of the C.N.E. as a symbol of

The Canadian Period (1870–1914)

Toronto's economic and material progress. In fact, in 1889, City Council had assumed all assets and liabilities of the C.N.E. and was responsible for the erection of all new buildings; consequently, City Council believed that "what was good for the C.N.E. was good for Toronto."[89] Through the years, as Toronto developed and expanded, so did the Exhibition grounds.

In the autumn of 1901, Toronto's mayor proposed a plan to enhance the Exhibition grounds by relocating the Woodbine Racetrack to Exhibition Park. Such a move would require the acquisition of more of Garrison Common from the military — in fact, the mayor even suggested that the City should take over all of the remaining military reserve from the federal government, including both the Old and New Forts. The Old Fort would be preserved by the City as an historic site, he promised, but Stanley Barracks would need to be moved to another location. Although the mayor's plan did not materialize, the writing was on the wall. By 1903, the City had negotiated an agreement with the federal government for the purchase of the garrison lands, including the Old and New Forts, from the Department of Militia and Defence. According to the terms of this agreement, the City agreed to let the Department continue to use the buildings it currently occupied, and as much of the land as it needed, until new buildings on a new site were constructed for the military's use. The City agreed to use the ordnance lands for "park and exhibition purposes" only, and to "properly care for" and preserve both the Old Fort and the military cemetery that lay between the two forts.

It wasn't long before the terms of this deal were tested. In 1905, in order to alleviate the annual traffic congestion at the western (Dufferin Street) entrance to the Exhibition grounds, the City considered the possibility of running a streetcar line from Bathurst Street to the east side of the grounds. In March of that year, the City engineer presented a proposal for the streetcar line route — right through the middle of the Old Fort! The plan would require the relocation or destruction of several historical buildings. At once, local historical, patriotic, and military organizations leapt to the defence of the Old Fort, beginning a battle that would rage through the next four years. An "Old Fort Protective Association" was formed to canvas support for the preservation of the fort, and to suggest alternate routes for the streetcar line. General Otter was one of its members, although he refused the honorary presidency since, as an employee of the Dominion government, he felt that it would constitute a conflict of interest.[91]

The Old Fort Protective Association appealed to the federal government to save the historic fort. Prime Minister Wilfrid Laurier neatly avoided embroilment in the issue. His reply to the Association was short and blunt: "The intention of the City authorities to cut a wide roadway and run a street car line through the Old Fort property is one to which the Government has no opinion to offer and which they must leave altogether to the citizens of Toronto." However, the defenders of the fort succeeded in winning the support of Minister of Militia Borden, as well as the federal and provincial Conservatives, and the Toronto Liberal press. Laurier finally reversed his position. He inserted a new condition in the deed of transfer, prohibiting streetcars through the fort, and requiring the City to restore Fort York to its original condition; otherwise, the Garrison Common lands would be returned to federal government ownership.[92]

In other respects, relations between the City and the military were often co-operative. The Old Fort buildings continued to be used by the military for storage of ammunition and supplies, and as dwellings for the fort's caretakers and their families. The City agreed to let the military continue to occupy Stanley Barracks for a period of five years, beginning in April 1908. The Royal Canadian Dragoons and the Royal Canadian Regiment at Stanley Barracks managed to co-exist peacefully, for the most part, with the C.N.E., the Exhibition Association even allowing the military to use stabling in Exhibition Park for its horses.[93]

Doris (Carter) Collins lived at Stanley Barracks around 1911–1912. She and her parents occupied one of the married quarters cottages in the southwest corner of the fort grounds. Doris's father, William Charles Carter, was a colour sergeant in the Royal Canadian Regiment. Doris was a child of three or four years of age when she lived in Stanley Barracks, but even as an adult, she could still recall Lieutenant-Colonel Arthur Steer of the Royal Canadian Dragoons (who was called "Shorty" because he was so tall); "Duffy" Diamond of the Royal Canadian Regiment, who was a particularly skilled marksman and partook in shooting competitions; and Farrier-Sergeant Simkins, known as "Old Simms." Simkins had

The Canadian Period (1870–1914)

three daughters; when his wife died, the other women of Stanley Barracks watched over his daughters.

The Carters' cottage was on the lakeshore, part of a block of three adjoined residences; to the young girl, the hill that descended to the water's edge resembled a veritable cliff — especially when a boy whose family lived in the adjoining cottage pushed her doll carriage over it. Like their predecessors, the British redcoats, a half century earlier, the soldiers of the garrison added military pomp and colour to the city. Every Sunday morning, in full dress, the troops would parade from Stanley Barracks, up Bathurst Street, to St. John's Garrison Church, trailed by the children of the neighbourhood.[94]

Canadians' respect for the Permanent Force seems to have increased during these years. In 1910, Colonel Sir Henry M. Pellatt decided to take his regiment, the Queen's Own Rifles, to Aldershot, England, at his own

The Royal Canadian Regiment and Royal Canadian Dragoons at Stanley Barracks, circa 1912–1914.

City of Toronto Archives, Fonds 1244, Item 718.

STANLEY BARRACKS

"General View of the New Fort, Toronto, 4 October 1913."

John Boyd, Library and Archives Canada, PA-060874.

personal expense, where they would train alongside British regulars who had already been under continuous training for six months. The regiment therefore was first sent to camp in Levis, Quebec, along with "nine of the most competent instructors in the Royal Canadian Regiment" (including four from Stanley Barracks), in order to have the members of the Queen's Own "hardened and brought to such a state of efficiency as will enable them to take their places creditably beside the British troops at Aldershot."[95]

In addition to the Permanent Force's instructional role, it had other duties. The 1904 Militia Act had given the Permanent Force prime responsibility for aid to the civil power. In November of 1906, a contingent of regulars from Toronto, made up of 173 men of the Royal Canadian Dragoons, Royal Canadian Regiment, and Royal Canadian Horse Artillery, was dispatched to Hamilton to quell the violence resulting from a streetcar operators' strike.[96]

CHAPTER THREE

The World Wars (1914–1945)

"EXHIBITION CAMP"

The success, and consequently the expansion, of the C.N.E. continued. By 1913, the Exhibition grounds stretched east to Strachan Avenue, and many new exhibition buildings had been constructed. The C.N.E. was officially opened by Prime Minister Robert Borden on August 24, who proclaimed 1913 to be "Expansion Year" at the Exhibition.

However, expansion came to an abrupt halt in 1914, with the outbreak of war in Europe. The military suddenly took precedence in Toronto life as never before. Ironically, well before anyone had anticipated war, 1914 had been declared "Peace Year" at the C.N.E., and the fair, scheduled to open on August 29, was intended to commemorate the signing of the Treaty of Ghent ending the War of 1812 one hundred years previously.[1]

Following the announcement that Canada was at war, rumours began to circulate that the 1914 exhibition would be postponed. The Exhibition Association vigorously denied such reports, and the fair opened as scheduled in late August. Daily newspaper accounts of the fair suggest that Torontonians were not about to let a war interfere with their enjoyment of the C.N.E. The Toronto *Globe* reported on September 2 that:"There was a repetition of war talk at the director's luncheon, but on the part of the public the fact that a war is in progress in Europe seems to be forgotten once the grounds are reached. It is a time to be relieved of those things that oppress the imagination, and the Exhibition is the place where this can be done. In spite of the spectre of hard times, money seems to be flowing freely."[2]

But shortly after the close of the 1914 fair, the C.N.E. grounds underwent a radical transformation. Recruitment, training, and mobilization of the Second Canadian Contingent was already underway; it was evident that it would continue into the winter months, at which time the military camp at Valcartier would no longer be able to provide suitable quarters for the troops. The military decided that, during the winter, all units would train locally, using armouries and other available buildings in the various district centres. On September 18, the Toronto *Globe* announced that the City was planning to offer the federal government the use of Exhibition Park as a winter training camp for the troops of Military District No. 2.[3]

Ottawa readily accepted the City's offer, and the conversion of the fairgrounds into a military camp was soon underway. All necessary alterations for the troops' accommodation were completed within three weeks. Furnaces were installed; bunks and sanitary facilities were designed and built; and an indoor rifle range was constructed underneath the grandstand. Most of the C.N.E. buildings would soon be put to use by the military, for some purpose or another.[4] The 15th Battery of Canadian Field Artillery, raised in Toronto in August as a component of the Second Contingent, found itself quartered in the cowsheds and stables, where stoves and double-tiered bunks had been hastily installed: "The accommodation was far from luxurious, but the troops had the advantage of being close to the attractions of the city, and during training were able to fire live ammunition at targets out on the lake."[5] Military District No. 2 was quite fortunate in having at its disposal the Exhibition grounds, with the many large buildings and stables, and the convenient location: close to the city, yet with ample space for drilling, and adjacent to Stanley Barracks and its facilities.

A description of Canadian war camps published in 1919 was unsparing in its praise of Exhibition Camp:

> [A]t Toronto winter-quarters of exceptional convenience were found in the capacious Exhibition Buildings — permanent structures of brick, steel and concrete which had

many advantages. Here, during the cold weather of 1914–1915, some 4,500 men were concentrated under the command of Major-General Lessard. The outdoor drill and route marching in the frosty days gave the men a good hardening, and by spring several battalions were beginning to have the swing of veterans. A curious effect of this outdoor life was found on occasions when entertainment of any kind was provided for the men in theatres or music halls of the city. After half an hour or so in the super-heated air required for an ordinary civilian audience, the soldiers would begin to cough. The unfamiliar temperatures had an uncommonly irritating effect on the throat. Frosty air was not troublesome."

Heavy snow could be a problem, however, preventing some activities which normally took place outdoors. Larger buildings such as the Transportation Building and the Machinery Hall enabled indoor drill; outdoor route marches continued throughout the winter.[6]

Troops marching past the Crystal Palace, C.N.E. grounds.

Photo by A.W. Barton, 1914. C 121-1-0-13-27, Archives of Ontario.

STANLEY BARRACKS

"Recruits learning to tie knots, C.N.E Camp," circa *1914.*

City of Toronto Archives, Fonds 1244, Item 747B.

"Guarding gates at C.N.E. military training camp," 1916.

City of Toronto Archives, Fonds 1244, Item 773.

The World Wars (1914–1945)

"*C.N.E. camp barracks before lights out,*" circa *1914–1915.*

City of Toronto Archives, Fonds 1244, Item 777.

A lecture course was provided for the troops at the camp. It covered such topics as tactics, topography, operations by night, engineering service in the field, patrols and patrolling, and military law. A library containing 1,100 volumes was available for the use of the troops, and the military Y.M.C.A., located within the grounds, provided movies, concerts, and educational lectures. Christmas at Exhibition Camp was celebrated with a "continuous program of amusements" for the troops in the Dairy Building.[7]

Health and sanitation were major concerns: in fact, the daily inspection reports submitted by the Camp Field Officer of the Day were concerned largely with the cleanliness of the quarters, and with the sanitary storage and preparation of food. Exhibition Camp included a gymnasium and four hospitals. During the course of that first winter, a few cases of pneumonia developed in the camp; more serious, however, was the outbreak of spinal meningitis in February 1915, which resulted in one death. Thanks to renewed exertions on the part of the medical officers, and the assistance of the Pathology Department of Toronto's School of Medicine, an epidemic

"Soldiers shaking and airing blankets in the Exhibition Camp, 13 March 1915."

John Boyd, Library and Archives Canada, PA-061389.

"Cavalry train, C.N.E. camp," passing by the rollercoaster, between 1914 and 1918.

City of Toronto Archives, Fonds 1244, Item 777J.

was averted. And while the weather may have forced the minister of militia and defence, Major-General Sam Hughes, to temporarily relinquish the camp at Valcartier, the principles he had advocated there could be revived in the new camps. In November 1914, Hughes visited Exhibition Camp, and addressed the troops about the virtues of temperance.[8]

The following winter, the Exhibition grounds were used again by the military as a camp, this time housing nearly ten thousand troops. The military continued to use the Exhibition buildings and grounds, either

The World Wars (1914–1945)

"*35th Battalion doing exercises in the Exhibition Grounds, 11 September 1915.*"

John Boyd, Library and Archives Canada, PA-071663.

to house and train troops about to be sent overseas, or to facilitate their demobilization upon their return to Canada, until July 1919. Despite the war, and the military use of the buildings during part of each year, the annual C.N.E. was able to take place as scheduled. C.N.E. planners chose a military theme for the 1915 fair, and 1915 was proclaimed as "Patriotic Year." The C.N.E. was able to capitalize on the military theme, and on the troops stationed at Stanley Barracks. A description of the fair in the Toronto *Globe* promised that "All branches of the Exhibition, as arranged this year, will harmonize and blend into one grand outburst of patriotic fervor.… No doubt the model military camp will attract thousands of visitors, a great many of whom have relatives at the front. In this camp will be seen a detachment of the Royal Canadian Dragoons, Artillery, Royal Canadian Engineers, Royal Canadian Regiment, including detachments for service at the front." The 1915 Exhibition would also feature displays of "Bursting shrapnels and bombs," "war trophies taken from the Huns on the battlefield," and "Blood-stained and torn clothing worn by soldiers in the trenches." But while seemingly profiting from the military presence as a draw for greater attendance numbers, the C.N.E. in fact assisted the military by setting up a recruiting station on the grounds during the fair.[9]

"Visitors to the 35th Battalion trenches, C.N.E., 1915."

John Boyd, Library and Archives Canada, PA-022593.

"Soldiers getting out of their trenches in the Exhibition Grounds, 11 September 1915." Note the C.N.E. visitors observing the exercise.

John Boyd, Library and Archives Canada, PA-071661.

The World Wars (1914–1945)

Due to the military use of the Exhibition grounds, some of the smaller fairs that took place annually on the grounds had to be cancelled, including the Motor Show and the Ontario Horticultural Exhibition. Other fairs and events went ahead as scheduled, forcing the military to adjust to the situation. Although troops still occupied the grounds in 1919, the scheduled Live Stock Sale took place as scheduled. A memo dated January 29 informed the commanding officer of Exhibition Camp: "… you will have to make the best arrangements possible to allow the necessary traffic of civilians interested in this sale — from February 5th to 8th — to enter the Grounds."[10]

Convenient as the Exhibition grounds may have been for the military, there were also difficulties. The military had to cope with problems caused by the camp's proximity to the civilian population. Members of the public with relatives in the camp hospitals tended to visit the hospitals at any time of the week; consequently, visits to Exhibition Camp by the public were restricted to Saturday and Sunday afternoons, which were the established visiting hours for the camp. Taxi cabs were also barred from the grounds, as soldiers were becoming "mixed-up with these taxi-cab drivers."[11]

"Visitors' Day, C.N.E. Camp," circa 1915.

City of Toronto Archives, Fonds 1244, Item 777H.

STANLEY BARRACKS

"Personnel of the Cycle Corps and Nursing Sisters leaving Exhibition Camp for overseas service, 15 May 1915."

John Boyd, Library and Archives Canada, PA-061452.

"Signallers in the Exhibition Camp and two goats, 24 March 1915." Note the proximity of the rollercoaster. The Dragoons' stables, housing approximately one hundred horses, were located in the northeast corner of the fort, right beside the C.N.E. rollercoaster. When the annual fair was underway, the rollercoaster provided good noise training for the horses.

John Boyd, Library and Archives Canada, PA-061413.

The World Wars (1914–1945)

For the most part, however, the population of Toronto seemed to adjust well to the presence of a military camp in the middle of their city. The members of the Toronto Women's Patriotic League knitted mufflers, socks, and caps for the men at Exhibition Camp; the Ontario Motor League voluntarily placed seven hundred automobiles at the disposal of the commanding officer of the camp, and League members volunteered to undertake machine transport drill in the transportation of troops and supplies.[12]

"Munitions workers parade at C.N.E. Grandstand," circa *1915.*

City of Toronto Archives, Fonds 1244, Item 858.

The 1916 C.N.E. featured special events such as a "Model Military Camp," which was set up west of the Transportation Building. At the camp, fair visitors could observe daily drill, bayonet exercises, and trench defence and attacks. Meanwhile, on the waterfront, a "Naval Demonstration" took place from 5:45 to 6:30 p.m. daily, featuring "Combat between submarine and Motor Patrol. Bomb dropping from Aeroplane. Submarine mines. Torpedoes in action." And again in 1917,

"C.N.E. Midway game featuring caricatures of Kaiser Wilhelm," circa 1914–1918. Other midway attractions included: Mazeppa, the Horse with the Human Brain; Dolletta, the Tiniest Mother on Earth; California Frank's Wild West Show; the "Globe of Death"; and a cannibal show.

City of Toronto Archives, Fonds 1244, Item 880.

"'Sticking Germans' in the Exhibition Grounds, Toronto, 22 January 1916."

John Boyd, Library and Archives Canada, PA-072491.

The World Wars (1914–1945)

"Soldiers napping, C.N.E. camp," July 1916.

City of Toronto Archives, Fonds 1244, Item 781B.

the annual fair celebrated and promoted Canada's war effort through a variety of military displays, including demonstrations of "bayonet and trench work" and "bombing on the lake front," while also commemorating the "semi-Centennial of Canadian Confederation."[13]

In 1919, Exhibition Camp functioned as a demobilization centre for the returning troops. Inspection reports for that year show that the number of guards stationed throughout the camp was reduced. The end of the war also apparently brought about some slackened conditions in the camp, especially in terms of quality of rations. One soldier attempted an anonymous appeal to the GOC of Military District No. 2. "[The food] is 50% worse now then [sic] the armistice was signed," he wrote to General Gunn. "It is not fit for cattle. I like the Army life fine myself, but would put more ambition into my work if properly fed.… Sir, seeing that the War is over, I think things should be a little better down here." Even Royal Canadian Dragoon prisoners in detention voiced complaints about the quality of the rations allotted to them.[14]

"C.N.E. Waterfront," February 3, 1919. Stanley Barracks is visible across the water.

City of Toronto Archives, Fonds 1244, Item 1733.

THE INTERNMENT OF "ENEMY ALIENS"

In April 1918, the following anonymous letter was received by the prime minister:

> I have just heard that *one* Major or Sargent [sic] Major at Ex. Camp. *Toronto* has a German Wife or one born in Germany and he has a lot of say at the Camp. This woman is at the camp quite a bit, she tells people she is English. I for one don't just like some things I see. So for my countrys sake I thought it best to put some one wise. Surly [sic] some other man could take his place. Remember Russia what a German wife did there. Don't trust any German wives these days.

The prime minister's office took this letter very seriously, as it did the hundreds of similar letters and complaints it received from anxious

Canadians during the war. The letter was immediately brought to the attention of the chief commissioner of police in Ottawa, as well as the district intelligence officer for Military District No. 2.[15]

From the start of the war, tensions were running high in many Canadian communities, as suspicions were raised over the loyalty of German-Canadians and other immigrants from nations now at war with Britain and her colonies. Anyone receiving mail from any of these nations, or even speaking with a German accent, was likely to become the target of the wartime fears and anxieties of his or her neighbours. Such anxieties, however exaggerated and misplaced they may have been, were given official sanction in August 1914 when Ottawa decided to impose restrictions on those deemed to be "enemy aliens": Canadians who were of German, Austrian, Hungarian, or Turkish ancestry, as well as those of Ukrainian descent from the provinces of Galicia and Bukovyna, which were under Austrian rule. The justification given for the government's policy toward enemy aliens was the possibility that German or Austro-Hungarian reservists might return to Europe to aid the enemy war effort, or, alternately, would support the enemy's cause by remaining in Canada and attempting acts of sabotage. The government's actions were also a response to economic depression in the nation and the prospect of increased unemployment in the upcoming winter season (enemy aliens would almost certainly be the last to be hired, or the first to be laid off; at least if they were interned, government officials pointed out, they would be housed, clothed, and fed for the duration of the war). But also, and perhaps most of all, Ottawa's enemy alien policy was formulated in response to the suspicions and prejudices of the Canadian public.[16]

An Order-in-Council of October 28, 1914, authorized the appointment of civilian registrars in major urban centres, who would act under the supervision of the chief commissioner of the Dominion police. All enemy aliens were required to report to the nearest registrar, and forbidden to leave the country without a permit issued by the registrar. The registrar could also decide to intern an enemy alien, who then would fall into the custody of the Militia Department. In Toronto, Judge Emerson Coatsworth was appointed "Registrar of Enemy Aliens" in November. A registration office was set up on Adelaide Street, and placards were posted

STANLEY BARRACKS

throughout the city and within a radius of forty kilometres outside the city limits, ordering all Germans, Austrians, Hungarians, and Turks to register as enemy aliens. The Toronto *Globe* reported in its December 22 edition that: "Alien Enemies are obeying the call of the registrar and seem to be quite eager to get their names down. The registration office on Adelaide Street West is besieged daily, a crowd of men being jammed against the door like the entrance to a popular show." This apparent "popularity" of registering one's name with the registrar can hardly be read as enthusiasm for this program on the part of those who had been classified as enemy aliens; they knew that, by law, if they failed to register as instructed, they could be interned. During the course of the war, eighty thousand enemy aliens registered in Canada. Of these, 8,579 men, 81 women, and 156 children would be interned in camps throughout Canada until the end of internment operations in June of 1920. Of the 8,579 internees, 5,954 were registered as Austro-Hungarians (including Croats, Ruthenians, Slovaks, Czechs, and Ukrainians), 99 as Bulgarians, 2,009 as Germans, 205 as Turks, and 312 were registered under the category of "Miscellaneous." Of the total, 3,138 could be legally classified as "prisoners of war" — meaning they had been captured "in arms" or belonged to enemy reserves. The rest of the internees were civilians, who, under the Hague Regulations, negotiated at the international Hague Convention in 1907, became subject to internment if the government considered them to be "agents" attached to an army, or if they engaged in activities that could be considered to be in service of the war. The director of Canada's internment operations, Major-General Otter, admitted after the war that the tendency of municipalities to simply want to "unload" their indigent populations resulted in the internment of a significant number.[17]

Seventy-one-year-old William Otter had been brought out of retirement to take on the position of director of internment operations. Offered the job on October 30, along with a salary of $5,000 (in addition to his military pension), he began work two days later. As the chief administrator of the internment program, Otter would be responsible for the accommodations, rations, and employment of the internees. Otter quickly established an office in Ottawa, manned it with a staff officer, a supply officer, and an accountant. (By 1916, this small staff would

These posters, demanding the registration of "enemy aliens," were posted in several languages throughout the city of Toronto in 1914. Creator unknown.

C 233-2-7-0-309, Archives of Ontario War Poster Collection.

increase to forty employees.) Next, Otter proceeded to search for suitable buildings and sites throughout Canada to use for internment, while also arranging with the Militia Department for a commandant and troops to administer each of the internment stations that were set up. The internees were considered prisoners of war, not convicts or criminals, and as such they were subject to the rules of the Hague Convention of 1907, which entitled them to the same standards of quarters, food, and clothing as was provided to Canadian soldiers. Jails or prisons could not be used as internment centres. Otter found a variety of sites to use, including local exhibition grounds and army barracks. At one point during the war there would be a total of thirty-two internment stations across the nation. In most cases, wire fencing was placed around the buildings, creating at least the appearance of a prison-like atmosphere.[18]

STANLEY BARRACKS

As early as August 1914, the Military Council in Ottawa had begun looking for a suitable facility for the internment of reservists in Toronto. The site suggested by the GOC, Military District No. 2, was Stanley Barracks, both because of its convenience and security: "Recommend portion Stanley Barracks. Troops for guards always there, easy to superintend, supply, etc." This choice of location was approved, and by September work had begun to convert Stanley Barracks into an internment station. The GOC reported on the progress: "Re internment Stanley Barracks. Possible to provide accommodation for eighty. Will take four weeks or more to complete arrangements. Electric wiring and fencing can be done in ten days, but bars will take some time, work will be hastened as fast as possible." And there definitely was no time to waste. As early as September 7, a German reservist was being escorted from Orangeville to Toronto to be "confined at Stanley Barracks."[19]

Of course, not all of Stanley Barracks could be spared for internment. The building designated for internment was the cavalry quarters, or the "West Block" — the privates' barracks on the west side of the fort, originally known as Range No. 2, which had a capacity of ninety men. A plan of Stanley Barracks, drafted by Lieutenant H.J. Burden in 1915, labels Range No. 2 as the "Prison Block." The 1915 plan also indicates that a "Prisoners Yard" had been laid out and enclosed in the southwest corner of the fort, between the officers' quarters and the new hospital.[20]

During the war, Stanley Barracks functioned as a "Receiving Station," rather than a full-fledged internment camp. Receiving stations served as transit centres for internees en route to more permanent quarters. This was most likely due to the limited capacity of the internment quarters at Stanley Barracks. Weekly reports issued regarding prisoners of war at Stanley Barracks show the number of internees fluctuating frequently, sometimes even weekly. A report issued in mid-October indicates that there were already seven prisoners at Stanley Barracks, three of them reservists. Two months later, the cavalry quarters were filled to capacity, and the general officer commanding of Military District No. 2 reported to Otter: "Ninety-three prisoners of war in Stanley Barracks. No room for more."[21]

The weekly reports that were issued list most of the internees at Stanley Barracks as "Austrian" or "Hungarian." They were "captured" in various

The World Wars (1914–1945)

German prisoners of war ("enemy aliens") temporarily interned at Stanley Barracks during the First World War. "Freedom of movement within the confines of the wire enclosure was always permitted at reasonable hours ..." stated director of internment operations William D. Otter in an interview for the Sunday World.

City of Toronto Archives, Fonds 1244, Item 867.

places: some in Toronto, others in towns such as Thorold, Hamilton, Brampton, or Niagara Falls, before being taken to Toronto. The internees often would be transferred from Stanley Barracks to internment sites such as Fort Henry or the camp at Kapuskasing.[22]

Otter personally inspected the Stanley Barracks internment station on November 13, 1914. Shortly thereafter, he requested that the commanding officers of the internment sites submit reports describing the internment facilities. The report submitted by Military District No. 2 supplies a fair amount of information about the operation of, and conditions in, the internment centre at Stanley Barracks. The presence of troops at Stanley Barracks provided a ready supply of guards. Five officers and 150 men were placed in charge of the prisoners. These guards were changed every three weeks, and their duties were distributed among different corps of the Toronto Garrison. The prisoners' accommodations consisted of cots placed four feet apart in a barrack room with one mattress and three blankets allotted to each prisoner. The general condition of the prisoners' private clothing was described as "Good"; the prisoners also were issued additional clothing by the government, namely boots, underwear, socks, shirts, mitts, caps, and coats. Rations were supplied by contract, at a cost of fifty cents per man per day. Breakfast consisted of: "porridge, bacon or sausage, potatoes, bread and butter, tea or coffee"; lunch was: "Stew or hash, potatoes, bread and butter, tea, tapioca"; and for dinner the prisoners were served: "Roast, 2 vegetables, pie or pudding, tea or coffee."[23]

The job of director of internment operations, and the scattered location of the internment camps, required General Otter to travel across the country many times throughout the course of the war for inspections. Otter, who had always been known for his administrative skills, was diligent, even painstaking, in his attention to detail. He inspected each internment station every three to four months. A meticulous record-keeper, he kept track of his daily activities and expenses, both business and personal, in tiny pencilled lettering in pocket-sized diaries. At each station visited, he made notes on the staff, troops, prisoners, condition of the quarters, rations, clothing, and discipline. When he found that the rate the contractor in Toronto was charging to supply rations to the internees was too high, he gave attention to the matter over the next several months as he tried to resolve the situation.[24]

By the terms of the Hague Regulations, POWs' personal belongings remained their property; however, they were not permitted to retain money or items that might facilitate their escape. Consequently, upon their arrival at an internment station, all money and jewellery was at once taken from the internees, and the money deposited in a "Prisoners of War Trust Fund" savings account at the Bank of Nova Scotia; jewellery items were locked in a safety vault. The amounts of money confiscated from each internee were listed for Otter's records. But despite Otter's efforts to keep track of the finances collected from the prisoners, it seems that this was one of the most vexing problems of the administration of the Stanley Barracks internment station. One of the outstanding events of the internment years at Stanley Barracks was the disappearance of several thousand dollars' worth of cash and valuables confiscated from the prisoners during the December 1914 to January 1915 period. No one was charged in the matter, as no records could be found.[25]

It appears that, afterwards, the administration tried to tighten up on financial matters. When a German prisoner at Stanley Barracks wrote to Lieutenant-Colonel Elliott at the military headquarters in Exhibition Camp, complaining that he had not received a $10.00 money order that had been mailed to him, Elliott promptly instructed the officer in charge of prisoners at Stanley Barracks to investigate: "Please let me know about this as it is most important that all monies of prisoners of war should be properly looked after."[26]

Other matters with which the administration had to concern itself included constant written requests from prisoners, pleading their innocence, and requesting release; co-ordination between the internment station and the registrar's office; and the hiring of interpreters to translate the internees' mail. Wives and other visitors were allowed to "interview" the internees, although visits were limited to one per month. One unusual and disturbing incident at Stanley Barracks was the death of a Turkish prisoner, necessitating a board of inquiry. After hearing the testimonies of the medical officer and of the officers in charge of the prisoners, the board ruled that the death was due to "natural causes, namely, 'pneumonia.'"[27]

In June 1915, registration was deemed "completed" by the office of the minister of justice, which had been responsible for internment since February 1915. The Toronto registration office, among others, was closed, and the registrar was dismissed from his duties. The Stanley Barracks internment station also did not last throughout the duration of the war. Otter's report lists the official closing date of the Toronto Receiving Station as October 2, 1916. Several other receiving stations and internment camps closed in 1916 and 1917. This may have been partly due to a desire to increase the administrative efficiency of the camps, but also was largely a result of the increasing manpower crisis in Canada. Prime Minister Robert Borden's increased military commitment of 1916, followed by the Military Service Act of 1917, which implemented conscription, quickly increased the number of Canadian men being recruited and sent overseas. This meant a reduced number of troops were available to guard the camps, and also created a labour shortage in Canada. No longer feeling as compelled as before to provide food and shelter for those of foreign descent, knowing their chances of finding employment were much better now, Ottawa began to wind down the internment program. Before the war's end, several thousand internees were released on a parole system which required that they sign a statement of loyalty to Canada and of obedience to Canada's laws, and that they report periodically to the nearest police authority. For others, internment continued until 1920.[28]

In 1998, the Ukrainian Canadian Civil Liberties Association and the Ukrainian Canadian community of Ontario, in co-operation with the Ukrainian Canadian Foundation of Taras Shevchenko, placed a plaque at the last remaining building of Stanley Barracks, to help ensure that this darker chapter of the New Fort's history would not be forgotten.

BETWEEN THE WARS

In 1908, the City of Toronto had agreed to let the military continue to occupy Stanley Barracks for a period of five more years. By 1918, the military had still not moved out of the barracks, nor had the agreement between the federal government and the City been renewed. The Old Fort, meanwhile, had not been restored to its original condition and preserved as an historic site, as the federal government had specified that the City was required to do when it transferred the Garrison Common lands to the City. Thirteen cottages within the Old Fort still housed tenants: military families who paid an annual rent of $1.00 per year each to the City Parks Department. Apparently the outbreak of war and subsequent military occupation of the whole of the Exhibition grounds had made the military's continued presence in Stanley Barracks a moot point, but now, with the war ending, City officials turned their attention back to the matter of Garrison Common. The Department of Militia and Defence asked for an extension of their use of Stanley Barracks and Garrison

Common in order to complete demobilization. A new agreement was drafted, granting the military use of "the Stanley Barracks portion of the Garrison Commons" for one year, for a rental fee, beginning June 1, 1920. There were a few conditions attached — including that the gate between the barracks and the Exhibition grounds had to be kept open.[29]

However, when the agreed-upon one-year period came to an end, again, nothing was done, and Stanley Barracks continued to be used by the military. In 1927, the matter was taken up again, and the City renewed the federal government's lease of the Stanley Barracks property. This agreement would be renewed again in 1932 and 1935. The 1935 agreement stipulated that the lease would be extended on a year-to-year basis, until the City served notice of its cancellation.[30]

After the war, regimental headquarters and "B" Squadron of the Royal Canadian Dragoons had returned to Stanley Barracks. "B" Company of the Royal Canadian Regiment moved to Stanley Barracks, where the Toronto station of the regiment was permanently established. The Dragoons reoccupied the west barracks (Range No. 2) and the Royal Canadian Regiment was quartered in Range No. 1, on the east side of the fort. Fort York remained in use as married quarters.[31]

During the 1920s, Stanley Barracks returned to its former glory days role as the focus of Toronto social life. "It was here that all the [prominent] visitors to Toronto were entertained," recalled the daughter of RCR Lieutenant-Colonel Arthur Steer. "It was at Stanley Barracks that the daughters of the regiment were presented to the Governor General — the Canadian version of being presented at Court." Dinners and dances held at the barracks were grand events. A few days before Christmas each year, the officers of Stanley Barracks hosted the annual "Children's Christmas Tree"; officers took turns each year in the role of Santa Claus at this afternoon party.[32]

The Dragoons continued their Musical Ride, and also participated in horse shows at Toronto's Royal Winter Fair, as well as at fairs in other cities, including Ottawa and New York. In 1926, the Dragoons formed a Canadian Army horse show team to compete with European teams in jumping competitions. The team performed well. Particularly notable were two troop horses, "Sergeant Murphy" and "Bucephalus," which had been purchased by the army in 1920 at the going rate of $175 each. Bucephalus, named after a steed owned by Alexander the Great in 356 B.C., was actually a transport horse; but after it was discovered that he had a passion and a talent for jumping — Bucephalus "could clear a six foot fence as though he had wings" — he became a star. Ridden by Lieutenant-Colonel Reginald Symonds Timmis for nine years in international competitions, Bucephalus collected more ribbons than any other Canadian horse at the time. His winnings included the King George III Gold Challenge Cup at New York in 1927 and again in 1930, as well as a $5,000 military stake in Boston in 1929. Bucephalus, known as "Dick" to the troopers, was retired from the army in 1937.[33]

The Royal Canadian Dragoons' riding team consisted entirely of officers, mainly because only officers had the private income to enable them to afford to attend the many horse shows. In fact, a 1928 squadron report criticized Timmis and some other senior officers for being absent from the squadron for several months in a year while attending competitions.[34]

"*The musical ride of the Royal Canadian Dragoons, C.N.E., Toronto, circa 1920.*"

Photo by Pringle and Booth. Canadian National Exhibition, Library and Archives Canada, PA-060582.

The World Wars (1914–1945)

"Major R.S. Timmis, RCD, riding Bucephalus, Royal Winter Fair, 1930." Timmis joined the Royal Canadian Dragoons in 1912 and would remain with the force until his retirement in 1937. At Stanley Barracks in the 1920s and 1930s, Timmis was in charge of the Musical Ride. He also organized and starred in the RCD "Mounted Circus," was a member of the Canadian Army International Jumping Team, and held office in several equestrian and animal protection societies. His diaries, preserved in the Baldwin Room of the Metropolitan Toronto Reference Library, reflect his love of horses.

Reginald Symonds Timmis Scrapbook, Library and Archives Canada, PA-060156.

Like many of Stanley Barracks' previous occupants, Timmis found that the winters in Toronto could be harsh, and the officers' quarters not well suited for such cold weather. "Bitterly cold in my room," he noted in his diary for January 2, 1924. Two weeks later he wrote: "Had fire in room, because it's so damp." In February he made note of a "terrible blizzard" that left eight-foot-high snow drifts on the fort grounds. On most occasions, however, Timmis welcomed the snow, since sleighing continued to be a favourite pastime of soldiers stationed at Stanley Barracks. "Thaw. Very mild! Boo hoo! All sleighing off now for bit," he recorded on an unusually warm winter day in 1924. His entry for January 25, 1925, was straight to the point: "Rotten mild."[35]

The Dragoons' Musical Ride and horse shows suffered an unfortunate setback in February of 1927, when a fire broke out in the stables of Stanley Barracks. An eyewitness reported the following day that, "Eight horses … were burned or suffocated to death.… Twelve more were blinded and so badly burned that they had to be shot.… Thirty-four others, turned loose for safety, ran wild and riderless through the streets of Toronto.… This morning nine are reported suffering from smoke or injuries, and of these six may die."[36]

During these years, the usual difficulties arose between the military and the City concerning the conditions of the military's occupation of the barracks. The City insisted, per the terms outlined in the 1920 lease agreement, that the gate between the Exhibition grounds and the Stanley Barracks portion of Garrison Common be kept open, allowing vehicular traffic to pass through the west entrance of the fort. But military authorities closed the gate at night. Drivers complained to the City, and the City complained to the commanding officer of Stanley Barracks, Lieutenant-Colonel F. Gilman. Gilman explained that the custom was to close the west gate at Retreat (sundown) and reopen it at Reveille (sunrise), and though this may inconvenience the general public, it was nonetheless necessary to prevent unauthorized individuals from entering the barracks area at night. With the large quantities of government stores that were kept at the fort, and the limited number of troops available to guard them, there was no other option but to close the gate at night. "Another evil, which it is felt this gate being closed at night prevents, is bootlegging," Gilman added.[37]

The World Wars (1914–1945)

"Death's head caution sign for motorists at New Fort, (Toronto, Ont.,) 16 December 1922." A photo of this sign appeared in the Toronto Globe *with the following caption: "Summary justice for speed fiends is forecast in this placard — one of two placed yesterday near the entrance to Stanley Barracks, where Corporal Taylor was injured last week. Taylor's comrades give due and sufficient warning to careless drivers." (Toronto* Globe, *December 5, 1922, 13.)*

John Boyd, Library and Archives Canada, PA-084958. John Boyd, Library and Archives Canada, PA-084958.

In October 1922, eight-year-old Roy James Dymond, who lived with his parents in the married quarters at Stanley Barracks, was playing on the grounds. Finding an old container, he opened it, removed its contents and struck them with an axe. The container had held a detonator, which exploded when struck, causing the boy to lose two middle fingers and the thumb of his right hand. An investigation was held. The boy's father, a company quartermaster sergeant with the RCR, was offered reimbursement of the costs of his son's medical and hospital treatment by the federal government, but the man refused the payment, threatening instead to sue the Crown. This resulted in a flurry of correspondence within the office of the minister of justice regarding the liability of the Crown in this incident. Was the injury due to negligence of an officer or employee of the federal government, while performing his duties of

STANLEY BARRACKS

employment? Are the barracks in question the property of the Crown? (They were, in fact, the property of the City of Toronto by this time, but occupied by the Permanent Active Militia, and under the control of the officer commanding, Military District No. 2.) After legal consultations, the federal government determined it was not liable to pay compensation for the injuries sustained by the child.[38]

And still there was the threat posed by the continuing expansion of the C.N.E. When Mayor Foster was heard to remark that the requirements of the Exhibition may before long necessitate the removal of most of the buildings of Stanley Barracks, many Torontonians began to voice their concerns about the preservation of both the Old and the New Forts. The *Evening Telegram* featured an editorial that criticized Toronto for not preserving the historic landmarks of the city. Some of the buildings on the fort grounds, such as the "East Married Quarters," located on the south side of the barracks at the east end, were in such a dilapidated state that they were uninhabitable and had to be removed, but the main buildings were in good condition. The *Evening Telegram* pointed out that Stanley Barracks' stone buildings "are about the most substantial structures in Toronto today. The original main buildings are still intact.

Aerial view of Stanley Barracks taken October 14, 1923.

John Boyd, Library and Archives Canada, PA-086347.

The World Wars (1914–1945)

The outer walls are of stone three feet thick and the inner walls of brick sixteen inches thick. The rafters are split logs and so substantial are these structures that no settlement has taken place in any of them, not even a crack in any of the walls...."[39]

In late 1926, the C.N.E. Association, seeking the development of the eastern Exhibition grounds (including the construction of a new roadway, Jubilee Boulevard, to serve as a new eastern entrance to the grounds), asked the City to serve notice upon the military authorities to vacate Stanley Barracks as soon as possible. Informed about this, and that it would entail the removal of several Stanley Barracks buildings — the engineer stores and workshop, a block of stables, and the riding school — Lieutenant-Colonel Walker Bell, commandant of Stanley Barracks, enquired if substitute accommodation to replace the buildings removed would be provided. The question was referred to the C.N.E. Association, who offered the military the use of "certain barns in our Live stock section, which is not too far removed from the Barracks."[40]

This was hardly an optimum solution for the military. Things seemed at a standstill, until February, when the mayor learned that the City of Hamilton was making inducements to the military to transfer the troops

Aerial view of Stanley Barracks gates and buildings to the south of the gates.

John Boyd, Library and Archives Canada, PA-086346.

at Stanley Barracks from Toronto to Hamilton. The mayor ordered that a meeting be set up between the commissioner of parks, the city solicitor, the president of the C.N.E., and Colonel Bell at the earliest possible date, in order to work out a compromise solution that would allow the continued military occupation of Stanley Barracks, without disrupting the improvements that the C.N.E. Association wanted to make at the eastern end of the Exhibition grounds. The meeting was held in the mayor's office on February 22, 1927.[41]

The resulting negotiations led to a list of twenty-one points that constituted the terms of the 1927 agreement between the Department of National Defence and the City of Toronto regarding the Garrison Common. The military would be allowed to continue occupying Stanley Barracks for five years from the date of June 27, 1927. The agreement included a provision allowing the City to construct a seventy-five-foot-wide roadway through Stanley Barracks; and, in order to enable this, authorized the removal of several barracks buildings: the engineers' stores, the riding school, and the "Old Stables." The City agreed to re-erect the stables and riding school in a different location, and to create an "Engineers Compound" to take the place of the stores building. The City was also obliged to care for all the relocated buildings, and to repair the stables that were damaged by fire earlier that year. The C.N.E. would allow the troops of Stanley Barracks use of the arenas in the Coliseum and the Livestock Building when they were not in use; would provide a training ground for cavalry between Stanley Barracks and Bathurst Street, south of Boulevard Drive; and would allow foot drill by troops in the Coliseum when it was not being used by the C.N.E. The minister of national defence agreed to let the public use the roads that passed through the fort grounds during the 1927 fair — but the entrances and gates remained under the sole control of military authorities. The barracks area was to be fenced on all sides, which would facilitate troop drill in the fort grounds. Colonel Bell also offered to make demonstrations of troop training available to the public during the C.N.E. The work was completed between June and November of that year.[42]

The arrangement was not exactly ideal, or even convenient, for the troops stationed at Stanley Barracks. Events taking place in the Coliseum limited the times that the building was available for military use. However,

The World Wars (1914–1945)

Some of Stanley Barracks' smaller structures, June 20, 1924. The second white building from the left is the old Guard House.

John Boyd, Library and Archives Canada, PA-086628.

Panoramic view of Stanley Barracks, September 21, 1925. The officers' quarters is in the centre.

John Boyd, Library and Archives Canada, PA-087234.

it was a workable, and necessary, compromise, if the C.N.E. and the military were to continue to coexist on the Garrison Common, and they made the best of it. In 1932, the City wanted to extend Jubilee Boulevard to the west, and a new agreement was entered into with the Department of National Defence, for three years starting June 27, with the same basic terms as the 1927 agreement. In 1935, the lease was extended for another year, beginning June 27; after that, the lease remained on a year-to-year basis.[43]

Aerial view of the Canadian National Exhibition grounds, August 1929, by Alexandra Studio. Stanley Barracks can be seen very clearly on the right side of the photo. Alexandra Studio was owned by brothers Lou and Nat Turofsky, who were prominent Toronto sports photographers, best known for their 1951 photo of Toronto Maple Leaf Bill Barilko's Stanley Cup–winning overtime goal. Each summer during the C.N.E., the brothers spent their days at the Exhibition grounds, documenting the fair and the grounds.

Alexandra Studio, Library and Archives Canada, RD-000916.

The World Wars (1914–1945)

According to Ed Johnson of the Royal Canadian Dragoons, who was stationed at Stanley Barracks from May 1937 until the spring of 1940, relations between the C.N.E. and the military were excellent throughout that time. The troops were allowed to use the Coliseum ring and grandstand track for training programs and exercise rides. In return, the Dragoons performed the Musical Ride and other riding displays for the C.N.E. and the Royal Winter Fair, at no cost. The Dragoons' stables (for approximately one hundred horses) were located in the northeast corner of the fort, right beside the C.N.E. rollercoaster. When the Exhibition was on, the rollercoaster provided good noise training for the horses.

During the 1930s, the RCR occupied the main stone barracks building on the east side of the square, while the RCD were quartered in the barracks across the square to the west, near the rollercoaster. The regimental headquarters of the RCD were located in the north building (the former hospital), opposite the officers' quarters. Behind the RCR block were a clustering of smaller buildings — the tailor's shop, the shoemaker's shop, the quartermaster stores, and the sergeants' mess.

View of Stanley Barracks from top of the rollercoaster switchback.

Photo by R.S. Timmis, 1923. Toronto Public Library (TRL): 995-1-10-41b.

The men's barracks rooms were quite stark, with a coal-burning belly stove for warmth in each room, and wooden floors that had to be scrubbed every Friday night or Saturday morning for the Saturday morning inspection. There were about twenty men to a room. Uniforms were hung on pegs behind the men's cots, and a barrack box at the foot of each bed held each man's spare kit.

For the members of the Dragoons, winters were busy with exercise rides, barrack fatigues and dismounted training courses, and stable duties. Evenings were spent mostly cleaning and polishing their equipment. March to May were spent in mounted troop training, usually in the Coliseum ring in the Horse Palace, and at the end of May, the troops went on a three-day ride to Niagara-on-the-Lake, where they spent the summer under canvas, training the various militia regiments who attended camp for two-week periods. The Dragoons returned to Stanley Barracks at the end of the summer, in time for the Exhibition.[44]

Ted Shuter, stationed at Stanley Barracks with the RCR at this time, recalled:

> Sunday was too often a church parade, the Catholics and Protestants in separate lots (no other religions permitted). We Protestants solemnly trudged out the gate, out the Princes' Gate to Bathurst St. and north to the old Garrison church there. Back again to a huge meal, usually roast pork, it was a feast! … One of our first duties on arriving in Barracks was to patrol the perimeter fence, and man the gate to beat off the curious public attending the Exhibition, particularly veterans dying of thirst who wanted to visit our canteen.

The regiment's routine was occasionally altered by special duties, including serving as firing parties for funerals, or as guards of honour for events such as the annual opening of the Ontario Legislature.[45]

In February 1936, Major G.R. Chetwynd of the Royal Canadian Engineers made an inspection of the stables at Stanley Barracks. Finding the conditions to be "very unsatisfactory," he reminded the City that, by the terms of the 1927 agreement, the City was responsible for repairs, and asked that these be completed as quickly as possible, "as the condition of the horses is being affected." Apparently nothing was done, because Chetwynd contacted the City again about the matter four months later. Over the next several years, the military repeatedly complained to the City about work that needed to be done at Stanley Barracks: the roads, the parade square, the stable yard, all were in poor condition. The stables in particular were constantly in need of repair: they needed painting, the roof was leaking, and the floors and windows required attention. With each request, the City stalled, trying to find funds for each repair project. Finally in the spring of 1939, the painting of the stables became a top priority because of the upcoming royal visit scheduled for May 22. The royal party's route would pass just a few feet from these stables. The parks commissioner quickly arranged to have the painting completed in early May.[46]

In 1937, Lieutenant-Colonel E.L. Caldwell, commanding Stanley Barracks, notified the City that one half of the bronze gates at the western entrance (known as the "Memorial Gates") to Stanley Barracks would not close. He pointed out the potential danger: in case of a fire in the stables, the horses would have to be removed and released, as had been done during the 1927 fire. "On that occasion they spread through the Exhibition Grounds and Parkdale," he reported to Commissioner of Parks C.E. Chambers. "Besides the risk of the horses injuring themselves, which we wish to avoid, there is the certainty that they will damage your lawns and flower beds."[47] The City promptly authorized and completed the repairs.

But the problems were neverending. Lieutenant-Colonel Timmis complained to the City that civilians constantly trespassed through the barracks in their cars, despite the signs that were posted on both the east and the west gates stating that the road through Stanley Barracks was not a thoroughfare. Late one night, a careless driver smashed his car into the east gate. Timmis demanded that action be taken to have the driver pay for the repairs to the gate. The driver insisted it was not his fault, claiming that the gateway was not adequately lit. He wrote to his alderman for assistance in the matter, and even had the Canadian Legion appeal to the parks commissioner on his behalf. On December 23, R.E. Riley

STANLEY BARRACKS

wrote to Chambers on behalf of the Legion. Not only was the driver in question a Legion member, he pleaded, but he was a coal-truck driver who earned only a meagre income. Perhaps, Riley enquired, since it was Christmastime, he could be forgiven?[48]

Several months later, a second letter from Riley arrived on the desk of the commissioner of parks. "I never heard back from you," explained Riley. "I had assumed you had forgiven the man, but now he has received an invoice for the damages." Riley again appealed again to have the claim against the man withdrawn. Probably tired of pursuing the matter, Board of Control agreed to cancel the claim.[49]

Stanley Barracks from the water, circa *1930.*

Photo by M.M. Hicks. Toronto Public Library (TRL): E 1-8k.

The World Wars (1914–1945)

"C.N.E. CAMP"

1939 marked the sixty-first year of the Canadian National Exhibition. Toronto's Exhibition grounds now encompassed 350 acres of what used to be the military reserve. The annual fair opened in late August, as usual; the theme was "Transportation and Communications Year."[50]

In early September, Canada was at war once again. The City immediately offered the use of the Exhibition grounds and buildings to the federal government, and once again, the Exhibition grounds became a military camp. No rent was charged, but the federal government was to assume the cost of all necessary alterations, and, after the occupation, would be required to restore the grounds and buildings to their original condition. By December 1939, most of the C.N.E. buildings had been put to use. The Royal Canadian Artillery occupied the Dominion Government Building; the 48th Highlanders, Toronto Scottish, and Royal Canadian Ordnance Corps occupied the Horse Palace; the Royal Canadian Engineers and Royal Canadian Air Force were in the Coliseum and Livestock Building; and the Dental Corps was situated in the Press Building. There was equipment stored in the General Exhibits Building, a Y.M.C.A. in the Graphic Arts Building, and showers in the Horticultural Building. Restaurants and dining halls became messes. The dressing room of the grandstand was converted into an anti-gas instructional chamber.[51]

During the Second World War, the Coliseum, which had been built in 1922 for the Royal Agricultural Winter Fair and the C.N.E., became the Manning Depot, occupied by the Royal Canadian Air Force. "B" Company of the RCR moved into the Horse Palace, where they bunked two to a stall. "The stable aroma did not bother us after a few days," remarked Lieutenant-Colonel Ted Shuter, "but it did set us apart when we visited the city."[52]

The federal government paid for alterations needed at the Exhibition grounds to accommodate the troops. In September 1939, C.N.E. General Manager Elwood Hughes was appointed to the Defence Purchasing Board of Canada. In this role, he would take charge of Military District No. 2's expenditures in connection with the housing and feeding of Toronto military units. The board supervised the purchase of construction materials required for the military occupation of the C.N.E. buildings, and of equipment and food for the troops. The Royal Canadian Ordnance Corps would continue to handle military supplies, such as clothing and boots.[53]

Because of the role it was believed the annual C.N.E. could play in the war effort, the federal government insisted that the annual fair carry on as scheduled. Not only did the "Ex" bring in money, but it provided an opportunity to show off British manufactures and to support British trade. All C.N.E. exhibitors were asked to tie in their war work with their exhibits. The RCAF Manning Depot would continue to operate during the fair, so that the public could observe as recruits were tested and trained, and even have the opportunity to talk to the air force men themselves. In short, the Exhibition would serve as "a vast display of Canada's war efforts …" The C.N.E. Association jumped wholeheartedly at the opportunity to help the war effort. It was decided that the 1940 fair would serve as a "school for civilians," informing and reassuring visitors about Canada's war efforts, and enlisting their support. The theme of the 1940 Exhibition was "'Canada Prepared' For War — For Peace." The fair abounded with military-themed exhibits, including a display of war vehicles in the Automotive Building; Red Cross activities in the Red Cross Building; a Bren gun exhibit in the National Industries Building; and "Women's War Work" in the Women's Building. The quilting bee, a regular feature at the fair, would have a different twist this year: the quilters would be making air raid shelter quilts to send to Britain. Even the advertisements in that year's "Official Catalogue and Program" had a decidedly military flavour. Christie's ad proclaimed, "We Salute the Empire!," while the T. Eaton department store advertisement featured a colour illustration of a soldier, sailor, and aviator marching past the C.N.E.'s Princes' Gates. Attendance at the 1940 fair reached an impressive 1.6 million visitors.[54]

In June of 1941, the district officer commanding of Military District No 2 requested the City's approval to erect additional buildings at Stanley Barracks to provide for better accommodation of the troops: a kitchen and a mess to serve one thousand men, as well as an officers' mess, were needed. The City gave its approval. Latrines and washrooms were also added or expanded.[55]

The World Wars (1914–1945)

"Capt. A.C. Lyons [with recruit], Stanley Barracks, 10 November 1940."

City of Toronto Archives, Fonds 1266, *Globe and Mail* Collection, Item 70321.

While the federal government had agreed to pay for alterations and maintenance, there were still disagreements with the City over who was responsible for the cost of watchmen, workmen, and workmen's compensation. There were concerns that bayonet practice, which consisted of bayoneting bags stuffed with straw and tied to trees on the lawn north of the Bandshell, would damage the trees. In early summer the parks commissioner worried that the lawns damaged by military occupation would not be in "fit condition for use" in time for the opening of the C.N.E.[56]

When the 1941 fair opened on August 22, an article in the Toronto *Star Weekly* promised fairgoers "the biggest two weeks of war propaganda this country has ever seen." Special features would include daily military ceremonies and parades, along with RCAF and RCN displays, including a half-dozen naval ships on exhibit. The Department of Munitions and Supply mounted a special exhibit in the Electrical Engineering Building

STANLEY BARRACKS

Stanley Barracks during the Second World War, as seen from the entry gates.
C.N.E. Archives.

to show off Canadian war industry. A special four-thousand-seat stadium was built south of the grandstand to provide a platform for demonstrations by Canada's mechanized forces. There would even be rides for children — in military vehicles. "All through the day and evening the crowds will glow and thrill in constant awareness of Canada's armed might and of a nation at war, reaching its full stride," the *Star Weekly* assured its readers. The British government also took the opportunity to promote British war production, and prepared an exhibit to ship to Canada. Even the transport of the exhibit from London to Toronto was planned with the intensity of a military operation: "This great display will reach Canada despite the Hun and high water. Shipment will be made early through the Nazi sea ambush. Should this fail, a second shipment will start, and a third if necessary." It was hoped that this year's fair in particular would draw many American visitors, and demonstrate to

The World Wars (1914–1945)

"*Hitler's Funeral, Exhibition Camp, 9 May 1940.*"

City of Toronto Archives, Fonds 1266, *Globe and Mail* Collection, Item 65880.

"*Parade, Stanley Barracks, 10 August 1940.*"

City of Toronto Archives, Fonds 1266, *Globe and Mail* Collection, Item 67988.

STANLEY BARRACKS

them the strength and unity of the British empire in the face of armed conflict, as well as "Canada's virility in the midst of war."[57]

The 1941 theme, fittingly, was "Canada's Answer." In addition to the usual military ceremonies and displays, and the RCAF Manning Depot in full operation, visitors to the fair were able to enjoy daily performances by the United States Navy Band — appearing "By special permission of President Franklin D. Roosevelt" — and a "War Relics Museum," comprised of a collection of items from the front: a German aircraft that had been shot down over Britain; an Italian parachute; pieces of German U-boat equipment; and "relics" from the bombing of Buckingham Palace, Westminster Abbey, St. Paul's Cathedral, and the British House of Commons.[58]

Following the massive success of the 1941 C.N.E., twice the usual space was allotted for military displays for the 1942 fair, which would be themed "Canada's War Effort." But in the spring of 1942 it was decided to discontinue the C.N.E. for the duration of the war. The next fair would not take place until 1947. The Royal Agricultural Winter Fair was also

"*Red Cross female drivers lined up, C.N.E., 4 September 1940.*"

City of Toronto Archives, Fonds 1266, *Globe and Mail* Collection, Item 68684.

The World Wars (1914–1945)

reluctantly cancelled for the duration, or "until Hitlerism has been annihilated," as Winter Fair manager William A. Dryden explained to the city parks commissioner. As of May 1, 1942, complete, year-round occupation of the Exhibition grounds for military use was granted to the federal government by the City for the duration of the war, and six months thereafter. Yet this agreement did not do away with the constant problems of military–civilian co-existence. The local police complained that military authorities stationed in the Exhibition grounds were continuously speeding, driving carelessly, and parking illegally. There had been nineteen accidents on the grounds, in which five soldiers were seriously injured. The chief constable urged that the Exhibition grounds be closed to through traffic.[59]

At a meeting of the commanding officers of the three services in June 1943, it was decided to turn the Exhibition grounds into a closed camp. Military officials hoped that this would also help to solve a problem that had plagued the Garrison Common since at least 1849: "At the present time

Gwen Elliot was a member of the Canadian Women's Army Corps and stationed at Stanley Barracks during the Second World War.

C.N.E. Archives, Gwen Elliot Collection.

STANLEY BARRACKS

The CWAC softball team. A softball diamond was constructed at Stanley Barracks in 1943.

C.N.E. Archives, Gwen Elliot Collection.

women of easy virtue wander about the grounds in the evening, and also gangs of hoodlums from time to time have broken the globes on electric light standards and caused other damage which in the end the Services are blamed for...." City Council authorized the decision on June 30, 1943.[60]

Alterations to the Exhibition buildings and grounds continued to be made, as needed. In January 1943, the windows in the Manufacturers' Building were altered in order to render the building usable as a classroom and drill hall. That spring, a women's softball diamond was established at Stanley Barracks. The Department of National Defence requested and received permission from the City to demolish the Old Stables and the "Old Maintenance Building" at Stanley Barracks, which were in poor condition and considered to be fire hazards.[61]

With the end of the war in August 1945, C.N.E. Camp became a demobilization centre for troops returning from overseas. "Civvy Street

The World Wars (1914–1945)

"Group in front of Stanley Barracks Chapel, 10 August 1940."

City of Toronto Archives, Fonds 1266, *Globe and Mail* Collection, Item 67986.

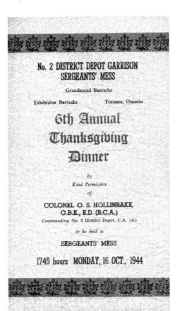

Cover of menu for the No. 2 District Depot Garrison Sergeants' Mess 6th Annual Thanksgiving Dinner, held on Monday, October 16, 1944 in the Grandstand Barracks at C.N.E. Camp.

C.N.E. Archives, Ed Anderson Collection.

STANLEY BARRACKS

Office" was set up in the rehabilitation facility at the camp in mid-1944 to help discharged soldiers reintegrate into civilian life and to assist them in finding employment. The men were warned repeatedly of various scams that were being perpetrated by hucksters who preyed on returning soldiers and advised them not to let their guard down, even though they were home from the war. A newspaper distributed aboard troop trains to provide instructions for dispersal procedures upon arrival at the No. 2 District Depot warned of "booby traps" that had been set for returning soldiers: "One lad bought a fish and chip store that didn't exist. Several have purchased land in which to build houses only to find, come spring, that their plots were six feet under water."[62]

The men were also warned of the shortage of civilian jobs, and encouraged to stay in the military until they could get a guarantee of

During the war, women were expected to take the place of men in factory work and keep essential industries going, while also remaining attractive and feminine, as demonstrated by the "Miss War Worker Beauty Contest" held at the C.N.E. Grandstand, July 18, 1942.

City of Toronto Archives, Fonds 1257, Series 1057, Item 1845.

employment elsewhere. They were also alerted about the postwar housing shortage, as well as the rising rate of venereal disease in Canada since V-E Day. ("You are coming home safely, why take the chance of getting yourselves wounded now," warned one military newsletter.) An additional concern was the considerable number of accidents that had been taking place as a result of the misuse of "souvenir weapons" brought back from the front.[63]

The military occupied C.N.E. Camp until June 1, 1946. It is estimated that during the Second World War, a grand total of twelve thousand troops had lived in the C.N.E. grounds. The annual Exhibition resumed in 1947. Unfortunately, the grandstand had been destroyed by a fire on April 14, 1946. The official souvenir program for the 1947 fair made note of the absence of the grandstand that year, but was also able to boast that "This year sees the revival, after six years of war service, of the Canadian National Exhibition, in new beauty, colour, and vigor, the embodiment of the spirit of a world facing a challenging future with clear eyes and a stout heart."[64]

CHAPTER FOUR

The Post-War Years (1945 to Today)

EMERGENCY HOUSING

After the war, the City of Toronto decided that it was now time to consummate the 1903 agreement and finally take over the entire military reserve. There was some confusion concerning the ownership of Stanley Barracks, however. J.P. Kent, the deputy city solicitor, pointed out that the most recent renewal of the lease of the Exhibition grounds and buildings (including Stanley Barracks) by the military had been on December 31, 1944, and that the time period specified in this lease ("for the duration of the war and a period not exceeding six months thereafter") had ended. The military was instructed to evacuate the Stanley Barracks buildings by January 31, 1947.[1]

In 1941, the Royal Canadian Dragoons had relocated to Camp Borden as an armoured cavalry regiment. After the war, the rest of the Permanent Force at Stanley Barracks began to move to the military training camp at Long Branch in Mimico. Mayor R.H. Saunders and C.N.E. general manager Elwood Hughes announced sweeping plans for the transformation of the Exhibition grounds. These plans included the demolition of Stanley Barracks, to make way for the construction of a new civic auditorium to accommodate conventions and cultural events. Seating fifteen thousand, the new auditorium would be "one of the finest on the continent," the mayor promised.[2]

However, there was a more pressing need. By 1944, major urban centres throughout the country, including Toronto, were facing a severe housing shortage, as living accommodations were needed for war workers, servicemen, and their families. Toronto authorities responded with the implementation of the Emergency Housing Program (EHP). The program was initiated with an agreement between the City and Wartime Housing Ltd. for the construction of one hundred housing units on City-owned land. The housing shortage only increased with the end of the war, and the influx of returning veterans. The scope of the EHP grew, more units were brought into the program, and by 1948, the City, through the EHP, was providing 1,350 emergency housing units on twenty-six different properties throughout the city and suburbs. Rental fees for the units were set at a low rate; as a result, the EHP soon was producing an annual deficit. As a solution, on May 1, 1949, management responsibility for the housing was transferred from the City Property Department to a private real estate agent named Harold V. Locke.[3]

A number of Department of National Defence buildings and facilities were converted into emergency housing, including part of the military training camp at Long Branch (on the south side of Lake Shore Boulevard), and the barracks of "Little Norway." Located at the foot of Bathurst Street near the lake, Little Norway had been built to provide housing during the war for members of the Royal Norwegian Air Force and Army Air Force when, after the German invasion of Norway in 1940, the Canadian government had offered the Norwegian military the use of facilities in Toronto for training.[4]

By the summer of 1946, some Stanley Barracks buildings — there were thirty-one buildings on the fort grounds at this time — had already been evacuated. The Dominion government gave authority to the City to use these empty buildings for emergency housing. Ottawa would contribute 50 percent of the cost of the conversion of the buildings to prepare them for civilian housing use. The remainder of the costs were assumed, albeit reluctantly, by the City. Emergency housing was "to alleviate a condition resulting from the war," pointed out Toronto's commissioner of finance to the mayor, "and is one which should have more properly been borne by federal funds, rather than by Municipal taxation."

The Post-War Years (1945 to Today)

Conversion required repairs and alterations to the buildings, acquisition of additional structures, and the preparation of education facilities — classrooms and equipment to furnish them, since, as part of the EHP, City authorities were required to provide school facilities for children living in EHP sites. With some minor adjustments to the officers' quarters building at Stanley Barracks, it was quickly outfitted to accommodate sixteen to eighteen families. A fence was erected to divide the fort's detention barracks, which were still in use by the military, from the rest of the Stanley Barracks buildings and premises. Plumbing and electrical work needed to be done, and locks installed on doors. By July 11, 1946, there were already several families living in Stanley Barracks.[5]

In the meantime, work began to convert more of Stanley Barracks into emergency housing units. It was hoped to be able to house up to ninety families at the fort. The cost of the work was estimated at approximately $100,000, of which the federal government would contribute $50,000. Rental prices charged for Stanley Barracks apartments ranged from $24.00 to $40.00 a month; there were also garages available for rent, at a rate of $3.00 monthly.[6] In February 1947, the commissioner of parks suggested the possible use of the detention barracks located on the east side of the Stanley Barracks parade square, and the mechanical transport building on the west, along with two smaller buildings, as emergency housing. He calculated that they could be converted into thirty-three to thirty-five apartments. By the end of April, there were 127 families residing in the Stanley Barracks emergency housing: 249 adults and 419 children. Never before had this many children lived at the New Fort. The barbed-wire fence that had stood on the north side of Lake Shore Boulevard through the Exhibition grounds had been removed, and there was concern that this created a hazard, making it possible for children playing around the barracks to run into traffic. The City paid to erect a chain-link fence between Stanley Barracks and Lake Shore Boulevard, enclosing the south side of the barracks grounds. The fencing was completed by mid-May.[7]

For C.N.E. officials, having a complex of buildings in the middle of the Exhibition grounds occupied by military troops during the annual fair had benefits as well as drawbacks: the opportunity to see uniformed soldiers and cavalrymen perform military drill provided an added attraction for fair visitors. But a complex that was inhabited by emergency housing residents was another matter. A proposal by the C.N.E. Association to erect a fence around Stanley Barracks was met with opposition from its residents. "We who are living down [here] do not like the idea we feel it would make it look like a concentration camp." But City officials, too, expressed concern about the unkempt and unclean appearance of the emergency housing apartments, especially since the City, at that time, was sponsoring a "Beautify Toronto" campaign.[8]

But the issues ran deeper. Later that summer, a group of Stanley Barracks' emergency housing residents submitted a list of complaints to the Board of Control. By this time, August 1947, there were 772 people living in Stanley Barracks emergency housing: 332 adults, and 440 children under the age of sixteen. The washrooms were only cleaned once a week, the residents pointed out. Coal piles lay uncovered within the fort grounds, giving easy access to children to play on them. The playground needed better supervision. They pleaded with the City to cover the hallway floors with linoleum, to insulate the water pipes, and to ensure frequent visits to the site by the health inspector. Sure enough, when the medical officer of health inspected Stanley Barracks, he found what he considered to be unsanitary living conditions: no covers on garbage containers, rubbish on the ground, numerous broken windows, and cockroaches. The fort's EHP residents also expressed concern that they would be greatly inconvenienced as crowds descended on the area during the annual Exhibition. And, as always, there were numerous complaints about the lack of sufficient heating during the winters in the Stanley Barracks buildings.[9]

As of May 1, 1949, the management and operation of Toronto's emergency housing premises, including Stanley Barracks, were transferred from the City Property Department to realtor Harold V. Locke. In addition to Stanley Barracks, the transfer included Little Norway, the military camp at Long Branch, North Camp at Malton, the former Boys' Home at 339 George Street, and one hundred wartime houses that had been erected on the fringes of city parks. By now, Stanley Barracks held 144 apartments for emergency housing, ranging from one to five rooms in size. The persistence of Toronto's housing crisis was clear in the fact that there were no vacancies: 144 families occupied the 144 units. The fort's residents consisted of 287 adults and 475 children.[10]

Locke hired night watchmen, who patrolled the fort grounds and submitted nightly reports to him, detailing any unusual activities that had gone on during their shifts. The buildings of the fort had all been designated by letters: A Block, B Block, C Block, and so forth. Fires were frequently reported in various buildings or locations, often in the garbage huts behind the buildings. Sometimes the fires were found to have been started by mischievous children, other times by a careless cigarette smoker. Such a large number of families, living in close proximity, and having to share certain facilities, including washrooms, invariably resulted in some problems for management. There were complaints about loud parties, or noisy washing machines in use late at night. Drinking and noise complaints seemed to be fairly common; the night watchmen came to expect these things, especially on Saturday nights. The Stanley Barracks emergency housing was often referred to in reports and correspondence as "the camp," a term which reflects the somewhat communal lifestyle of the residents. In May 1949, for example, the resident of Apartment 22 in "C" Block complained that women living in Stanley Barracks had a tendency to gather at "C" Block, sit on the doorstep, and talk late into the night. A tenant in Apartment A-4 voiced concerns that a male resident was seen at times carrying a billy club or a black-jack, entering the women's washroom at night, or wandering the hallway of the building partially undressed. On September 3, 1949, the night watchman on duty reported having to break up a craps game taking place in "D" Block. "Lots of money in it," he noted. During the C.N.E., residents complained of traffic congestion. There were also concerns about cars that were "travelling too fast around the roads."[11]

One night Harold Locke, along with his wife, paid a surprise visit to Stanley Barracks at 11:10 p.m., only to find that both the east and west gatemen had deserted their posts. The gatemen did not show up again until midnight. The incident was repeated three nights later, with the west gate watchman disappearing from approximately 11:15 p.m. until midnight.[12]

STANLEY BARRACKS

In October 1949, a resident of Stanley Barracks felt compelled to write directly to Mayor Hiram McCallum to complain about the poor living conditions at the fort, reporting broken windows, and no window screens; there were plenty of vermin, especially cockroaches and bedbugs; there were leaking taps, and his rangette was "constantly on the burn." And there were constant complaints, throughout each winter, about the insufficient heating, eliciting this exasperated response from a night watchman: "There are lots of complaints concerning heat situation premises are cold they say, and that is [what] we have to listen to at all times. However they are not suffering from any great exposure if keep their doors closed."[13]

Crime was also an occasional problem. A night watchman in January 1950 reported coming across a man, seemingly lost, wandering around the fort; he had a black eye and two large cuts on the left side of his face. He told the watchman he had been beaten up by four or five teenagers from Stanley Barracks. That same winter, Mrs. Pringle's grocery store was broken into in the middle of the night on two separate occasions. There were other occasional thefts and break-ins, some of them believed to be committed by residents of Stanley Barracks. Other times, intruders onto the property were blamed. A report submitted by the night watchman on November 11, 1949 stated: "We had about half dozen zootsuiters arrive at S.B., but they soon departed when I informed them to get off the premises." One night in April 1950, a "zootsuiter from Queen Street" was found with a concealed weapon in "O" Building. The weapon was identified as having been stolen from a Sporting Show held on the Exhibition grounds a few weeks previously.[14]

Toronto police were often called to Stanley Barracks to deal with such disturbances. In the summer of 1950, plainclothes policemen were dispatched to the fort to investigate suspicions of bootlegging in the barracks. The exasperated night watchman complained that dealing with the many maintenance issues and tenants' complaints was keeping him busy — too busy to have time to assist the police in their investigation.[15]

The Post-War Years (1945 to Today)

DEMOLITION

The City's plans to raze Stanley Barracks in order to allow the continued expansion of the C.N.E. were not forgotten — only delayed. The Emergency Housing Project had been but a temporary measure, after all, and City and C.N.E. officials were eager to close the housing and move on with their plans now that military had fully vacated Stanley Barracks and the City was fully in possession of the buildings and lands. City Council met and adopted a recommendation to set definite dates for the "progressive discontinuance" of Emergency Housing Projects throughout the city. The Stanley Barracks project, it was decided, was slated to be closed by May 1, 1951.

The process to evacuate the buildings began in 1950. By June, twelve families had been moved out of the "A Annex" building, and quotes collected for the demolition of buildings E, F, G, H, I, J, and O. However, many of the families resisted leaving Stanley Barracks, not having anywhere else to go. Some complained to their Members of Parliament, who in turn brought those complaints to the mayor. Residents were being *forced* to move, the mayor was told, without being given any assurance of new buildings or new homes to go to. Harold Locke, the realtor in charge of the EHP, was at a loss as to how to proceed. He commented to City officials that "The closing of Stanley Barracks without a doubt presents the most difficult problem that we have encountered up until this date. We have done everything in our power to convince the tenants that they must move." Locke tried offering the tenants alternate accommodations at other EHP sites that were still in operation, such as the ones at Malton, Long Branch, or GECO — the wartime munitions plant that had been converted into emergency housing after the war. But the Stanley Barracks tenants seemed unwilling to move.[16]

The situation turned into a public relations nightmare for the City. A headline in the *Globe and Mail* cried, "Barracks to be Razed, Families Must Move," above photographs of some of the affected residents: an eighty-four-year-old man and his wife; and a young mother with two toddlers. Neither family, the *Globe and Mail* reported, knew where they would go once they were forced out of their Stanley Barracks apartments.

The mayor's office also received mail from outraged citizens; one woman informed Mayor McCallum that the evacuation of Stanley Barracks, while the housing shortage continued, would be "one of the crimson blots on Toronto." Another woman appealed to the mayor, explaining that her son lived in Block "M" of Stanley Barracks with his wife and two young children, but they had nowhere to move to, as they couldn't afford to purchase a house. The mayor sent a lengthy response, explaining that they were doing all they could, but Stanley Barracks had only been intended to serve as temporary housing. With large numbers of people moving to Toronto from other parts of Canada, as well as from other nations, the City was unable to control the factors causing the housing shortage. In any case, he pointed out, housing was not a municipal responsibility.[17]

An article in the *Globe and Mail*, titled "Stanley Barracks Lights OUT," focused on one particular family, the Beattys. Mr. and Mrs. Beatty, along with their nine children, their dog, and their cat, had lived at Stanley Barracks for four years, paying a monthly rent of $38.00 for their apartment in Building "D." Russell Beatty, who worked as a machinist with the Massey-Harris company, had received notice to vacate the premises six months prior, but was unable to find another affordable home to move to with his family. The previous Monday, according to the story, Beatty returned from work to find his home in darkness. The following day, the water was shut off. The Beattys were getting water for washing and drinking from friends, and were living by candlelight, while the City continued to board up windows throughout the fort.[18]

The Toronto Board of Control reported that as of February 1, 1951, there were still seventy-three families in residence at Stanley Barracks. By summertime, all of the families would be evicted. Meanwhile, demolition of the buildings had already begun: that spring, two small stone buildings located in the southwest corner of the grounds, along with several wooden buildings, were torn down and removed.[19]

As the City proceeded with its plans for the redevelopment of Stanley Barracks, attention turned from the fates of the EHP tenants to the imminent demolition of what many Torontonians recognized as important historic buildings. Four main stone buildings still stood at the

The Post-War Years (1945 to Today)

Stanley Barracks during demolition, 1951.

Photo by J.V. Salmon. Toronto Public Library, (TRL): S 1-1222C.

fort, one on each side of the parade square: the officers' quarters on the south side, the old hospital building on the north side, and the east and west soldiers' barracks blocks. The recently formed City agency known as the Toronto Civic Historical Committee was consulted; the committee informed the City that it was agreeable to the demolition of all the buildings of Stanley Barracks, except for these four, which, because of their "historic and architectural importance," should be preserved. It recommended that these buildings be turned over to the Parks Service and operated as a museum, similar to Fort Malden in Amherstburg. The Board of Control concurred with the committee's recommendation.[20]

In the meantime, the eviction of tenants and the demolition of the auxiliary buildings continued. In August 1951 Building "R" on the north side of Stanley Barracks was vacated and demolished, along with adjoining buildings, by the Standard House Wrecking Company. "K" Building was closed on August 23. The following day the *Globe and Mail* reported, "Last Family Moved Out, K Block to Be Wrecked at Stanley Barracks," and included a personal portrait of the family in question — the Weirs — who, with their ten children, would be relocating to Emergency Housing in Malton. The article focused on the children, who expressed sadness at having to leave the barracks and the community that had sprung up there during the emergency housing years. A community hall in one of the buildings had been set up, where regular sports events had been held. John Weir had helped organize a boxing school for boys; there was also a girls' relay team, plus floor hockey, baseball, and racing activities for all of the young people living at the fort. Eighteen-year-old Mary Weir was interviewed. "The kids are all sorry to leave," she explained. "We could go swimming in the lake. There was always something doing. You couldn't want a better summer home."[21]

Throughout September, the City continued with the demolition of the smaller buildings of Stanley Barracks, including the garage, the chapel, the store, and frame additions that had been built onto the four large stone buildings.

While City and C.N.E. officials decided on their final plans for Stanley Barracks, concerned citizens began to voice opposition to any further demolition. A particularly poignant appeal was sent to the mayor from His Majesty's Army and Navy Veterans' Society:

> [We] are fully cognizant of the fact that for the past 35 years the Exhibition authorities have endeavoured tooth and nail to secure this property and NOT unlike HIROSHIMA wipe it completely off that portion of the Lakefront map. Fortunately in our opinion, the last two great wars have prevented this dire happening, to turn this historic spot into a Midway or some other form of cheap miserable entertainment for approximately two weeks each year.… [S]ince April 1st, 1884, this place has fully done its duty in helping to preserve the national existence of Canada, in teaching to safeguard

the blessings of peace by the skilful use of organization, administration, and the use of weapons, "lethal" perhaps, but not frowned on by the Volume of the Sacred Law. To descend from the sublime to the lower realities of life, this same Stanley Barracks, has been and will continue to be a source of greater Monetary value to Toronto, in any two weeks, compared with the profits of selling a few mildewed peanuts in a corresponding two weeks of Exhibition time. Therefore, Sir, we appeal to you to enlighten any or all personnel who are under the impression that the destruction of Stanley Barracks would bring Utopia to Ontario, or Toronto."[22]

Canada's governor general, Vincent Massey, even used the opportunity of his speech at the opening of the 1952 C.N.E. to support the preservation of Stanley Barracks. "I needn't remind anyone here of the part which these grounds and buildings have played in the two great wars to accommodate many thousands of members of the Canadian forces. Here, indeed, were great chapters in the history of the Exhibition. I believe there is now a feeling widespread and growing that we cannot afford to lose these none too numerous survivals of the past."[23]

Like an old soldier who had served his country well, Stanley Barracks should have been allowed to retire honourably. But this was not to be. In 1953, three of the remaining structures were razed, in order to create more parking spaces for the C.N.E. The huge wrought-iron gates of Stanley Barracks, two smaller pedestrian gates and the curved iron fences that flanked them, along with some of the stone from the demolished barracks, were purchased by a private developer for use in the construction of the Guildwood Village residential area in Scarborough. The gates, forged in the British Isles in 1839 and shipped to Canada in 1841 for use at the New Fort, would return to the Exhibition grounds in 1957, where they were displayed at the Guildwood Village exhibit at the National Home Show. The theme of Guildwood was "Your Gateway to Finer Living." After the Home Show, the gates were erected on Kingston Road in Scarborough, forming the entrance to Guildwood Village.[24]

STANLEY BARRACKS

The one remaining building of Stanley Barracks in the 1960s, surrounded by a sea of parked cars.

City of Toronto Archives, Fonds 1257, Series 1057, Item 744.

The York Pioneer and Historical Society urged that the last remaining building, the officers' quarters, be placed in the care of the Toronto Civic Historical Committee (which was already in charge of Fort York) for preservation. If turned into a museum, the committee argued, it would actually benefit the C.N.E. by serving as an attraction at the annual fair. Some proponents of the preservation of the Stanley Barracks officers' quarters, including A.D. McFall, president of the York Pioneer and Historical Society, and Lieutenant-Colonel W.W.G. Darling, president of the Royal Canadian Military Institute, suggested that the City consider establishing

The Post-War Years (1945 to Today)

a marine museum in the building, to display the naval history of Upper Canada, especially the War of 1812. Darling referred to the strip of land on which the Old and New Forts were located as the "royal mile of Toronto's history," and needled the mayor by pointing to the preservation of historic sites such as Sackets Harbor in the United States, insisting that Americans would never let a site of such historic significance be destroyed.[25]

The Women's Canadian Historical Society of Toronto wrote to the mayor in support of saving Stanley Barracks' one remaining building. Dr. Norman Found, a Toronto physician and surgeon, informed the mayor that if the building were destroyed, "I for one will consider it a sample of economic and historic vandalism." Historian J.M.S. Careless added his

Stanley Barracks' original gates were preserved and moved to the entrance of Guildwood Village on Kingston Road, in Toronto's east end.

Photo by Timo Puhakka, 2010.

voice to the protests, proclaiming that the demolition of Stanley Barracks' last building to make way for a C.N.E. parking lot would signify "the triumph of the automobile over every human value."[26] This time, the automobile did not win. By 1957, the Toronto Civic Historical Committee was at work restoring the one last building of Stanley Barracks, with the intention of turning it into a museum.

THE LAST BUILDING STANDING

> So many memories; for some of us it is sad to see just the one building sitting by itself overlooking the lake in the Exhibition grounds, brooding over the years that have passed.
>
> — Dorothy Steer Brasier, former Stanley Barracks resident[27]

In 1959, the officers' quarters building of Stanley Barracks was opened to the public as the Marine Museum of Upper Canada. The inaugural address at the August 26 opening ceremony was delivered by admiral of the fleet, the Earl Mountbatten of Burma, patron of the museum. Due to delays in restoration of the building, the opening actually took place later than anticipated; however, the Marine Museum was open for the 1959 C.N.E., and an estimated thirty thousand visitors toured the museum during the fair. No entry fee was charged, but a donation box was placed in a prominent location in the museum. Unfortunately, the box was robbed of most of its contents three days before the end of the Exhibition.[28]

Restoration costs were higher than had been anticipated; the building was in bad shape from neglect and alterations during its emergency housing years. Appropriations from the City coffers for Stanley Barracks restoration in 1957 and 1958 were exhausted by October of 1958. Restoration work continued after the 1959 official opening of the Marine Museum, and into the early 1960s. But the building was already finding numerous uses. In 1955, a Canadian Sports Hall of Fame was established and housed in the officers' quarters until 1957, when it relocated to the C.N.E. Press Building (the former Administration Building). When a new building was constructed on the Exhibition grounds in 1961 to house the National Hockey Hall of Fame, which had previously shared space in Stanley Barracks with the Sports Hall, both moved into the new building, which was located across from the Food Building. In 1993, the Hockey Hall of Fame moved to the former Bank of Montreal building at Yonge and Front Streets in downtown Toronto. Thirteen years later, the Hall of Fame building at the C.N.E. was demolished, leaving the Sports Hall of Fame without a facility. The collection was moved back into Stanley Barracks for storage. The Sports Hall plans to reopen at Canada Olympic Park in Calgary, Alberta, in 2012.

In 1960, the Toronto Civic Historical Committee (forerunner of the Toronto Historical Board, now called Heritage Toronto), which administered several historic sites around the city, including Historic Fort York, moved its offices into the Stanley Barracks officers' quarters, where it shared space with the Marine Museum. The building also housed a restaurant, the Ship's Inn. The Inn, which could accommodate sixty diners, plus an additional sixty in the summer on an adjoining patio, shared the basement level of the officers' quarters with museum storage rooms and workshops.

In 1998, after almost forty years in Stanley Barracks, the Marine Museum relocated to a restored 1930s warehouse building at Toronto's Harbourfront and was rechristened The Pier Museum. It only lasted a few years in the new location; by 2001, Toronto's maritime and naval museum had closed its doors for good.

Stanley Barracks' last building, however, has stood its ground. And, it appears, will continue to do so. The officers' quarters was recognized as a property of architectural and historical value when, on April 15, 1999, Toronto City Council designated the building as a "Landmark Heritage Property" under the Ontario Heritage Act, By-law 188-1999. However, the area has also been identified by the Exhibition Association and City officials as having development potential, and an appropriate adaptive reuse of the building was sought. Various ideas were offered; some suggested that Stanley Barracks was the ideal location for a museum of Toronto's military history.

In the fall of 2009, City Council, recognizing the need for hotel accommodations to complement the convention facilities of Exhibition Place, approved plans for the development of a proposed twenty-six-storey, three-hundred-room boutique hotel that would incorporate the last remaining building of Stanley Barracks. The City's Heritage Preservation Services were charged with monitoring the plans for the project, to ensure heritage concerns are addressed, including archaeological concerns. The history of the New Fort may have disappeared from sight over the years as the fort's buildings, one by one, were torn down. But the foundations remain underground, along with potentially thousands of artifacts that tell the story of Stanley Barracks and those who lived there. Archaeological assessments that have been done in recent years on the Exhibition grounds have revealed a significant number of historic features extant under the ground. Test trenches done in 2006 and 2008 east of the officers' quarters building located the stone foundations of the Range No. 1 enlisted men's barracks. The architect for the hotel developer, HK Hotels of New York, has proposed exposing and interpreting these features, as a way of preserving and incorporating some of the history of Toronto, and of Stanley Barracks, into the new hotel development.[29]

Surrounded now by the buildings and parking lots of Exhibition Place, its once vast grounds swallowed up by the development and expansion of Toronto, Stanley Barracks is nevertheless a striking and very real reminder of Toronto's British garrison and the role it played in the development of the city. While City officials and many citizens have felt that the lands reserved by the military hindered Toronto's physical growth, in times of crisis no one objected to the defence provided to the town by the garrison. Nor did anyone object to the other services and benefits provided to the town by the local military force, from providing firefighting services, to offering the entertainment of the Musical Ride.

Forts have been called the foundations of Canadian urban settlement. Whether established for military, political, or economic reasons, they have determined the patterns of settlement in Canada.[30] The establishment of the garrison at Toronto by John Graves Simcoe in 1793 paved

The Post-War Years (1945 to Today)

The officers' quarters of Stanley Barracks in 2010.

Photo by Jamie Maxwell.

the way for civilian settlement, and provided the settlers with a market as well as with defence. The defensibility of Toronto caused Simcoe to transfer the provincial capital to Toronto, boosting its population, as well as its status.

Toronto's forts also revealed basic assumptions about Canadian military thinking: that the main threat was from the south. In other ways, too, Toronto's garrison reflected national military policy. Historically, Canadians have tended to display uncertainty about the need for professional armed forces. Defence is costly and has been considered a luxurious commodity. Military spending and defence issues were almost always divisive, usually along already fragile French-English lines, and Canadian politicians have tended to opt for unity over military preparedness. After all, it was believed that Canada had few real enemies to fear, and, if worse came to worst, could rely on Britain's military forces for defence. Even the Canadian militia, while often hailed as the true defenders of the nation, tended to be regarded not so much as a realistic military force, but as a source of political patronage.

Consequently, Canadian military preparedness was often overlooked by Ottawa, except in times of crisis, when martial or imperial enthusiasm, or simply fear of war, captured public opinion and demanded that the government turn its attention — and its funding — to the military. These crises showed the need for military professionalism and preparedness, but once the crises had passed, the lessons which ostensibly had been learned were forgotten, forces were disbanded, and funding withdrawn. Canadians preferred an *ad hoc* call to arms over military preparedness.

The story of Stanley Barracks is important in this larger picture, for it is an illustration of Ottawa's attitude toward, and handling of, the military. From the time of Confederation, the military and its development has been of minor importance to Ottawa. Canada inherited the British military tradition, as it inherited the British garrison of Stanley Barracks; but both were treated with disinterest, sometimes even with callous neglect. Only in times of crisis, when necessity dictated (and public opinion allowed), did Stanley Barracks become an active and important centre. It was through such crises that a Canadian Permanent Force was given a chance to develop.

Ultimately, and predictably, civilian interests took precedence over military, and the military was forced to vacate Stanley Barracks and move into modern military camps and bases. While these camps may have been more practical to the modern military than the nineteenth-century barracks, they too were created in times of crisis and unusual martial spirit, or for political reasons.

Yet the importance of the military in the history and development of Canada is unquestionable. The story of Stanley Barracks is part of that larger history. Since its establishment more than 170 years ago, it has not only been a major player in the history of Toronto, but it is a part of the history of the relationship between Canada and its military forces.

NOTES

CHAPTER ONE: THE BRITISH PERIOD (1840–1870)

1. Carl Benn, *Historic Fort York 1793–1993* (Toronto: Natural Heritage/Natural History Inc., 1993), 22.
2. Edith Firth, introduction to *The Town of York 1815–1834: A Further Collection of Documents of Early Toronto* (Toronto: Champlain Society/University of Toronto Press, 1966), xx.
3. John Graves Simcoe to the Duke of Richmond, September 23, 1793, in *The Town of York 1793-1815: A Collection of Documents of Early Toronto*, ed. Edith Firth (Toronto: Champlain Society/University of Toronto, 1962), 61.
4. Benn, *op. cit.*, 65; C.P. Stacey, *Canada and the British Army 1846–1871: A Study in the Practice of Responsible Government*, revised ed. (Toronto: University of Toronto Press, 1963), 17.
5. Carl Benn, "Toronto's Forgotten Fort," (unpublished article), Fort York Archives (hereafter cited as FYA), File "Stanley Barracks — General."
6. Firth, introduction, to *The Town of York 1815–1834: A Further Collection, op. cit.*, xx–xxi.
7. "Extracts from a Report of a Barrack Inspection at Toronto dated 19 August 1840 from Messrs. Eaton & Elliott" (accompanying letter from R. Byham, Office of Ordnance to Inspector General of Fortifications,

November 2, 1840), Library and Archives of Canada (hereafter cited as LAC), W.O. 55, Vol. 875.
8. R. Byham, Office of Ordnance, to Inspector General of Fortifications, June 14, 1839, LAC, W.O. 55, Vol. 874. The province was unable to transfer the £10,000 to the ordnance storekeeper when requested to do so by the lords of the treasury, blaming "existing Financial embarrassments." The provincial secretary of Upper Canada, however, did acknowledge the debt. As contracts had already been entered into for the construction of the barracks, the necessary funds were taken from the military chest, to be refunded later from the provincial reserves. Chief Secretary Murdoch to Lieutenant-Colonel O'Donnell, Military Secretary, March 3, 1840, LAC, RG8, C Series, Vol. 592, 85–86.
9. "Memoranda upon the nature and value of Materials, as also on Labour in Canada from information in the Office of the Commanding R. Engineer," 1841, Metro Toronto Public Library (hereafter cited as MTPL), Baldwin Room; extract from *Globe Pictorial Supplement* (transcribed), December 1856, FYA, File "Stanley Barracks — General."
10. "Estimate of the probable expense of Constructing a Barrack Establishment at Toronto, revised for 300 Men, from the Plans & Estimates forwarded by Colonel Nicolls on the 28 December 1833 amounting to £22,853.6.7 ¼ ," London, February 28, 1839, LAC, W.O. 55, Vol. 874.
11. Sir John Colborne to Viscount Goderich, secretary of state for War and the Colonies, January 23, 1833, in Firth, ed., *The Town of York 1815–1834: A Collection of Documents, op.cit.*, 33; "Estimate of the probable expense of Constructing a Barrack Establishment at Toronto …," February 28, 1839, *op. cit.*; "Memoranda upon the nature and value of Materials as also on Labour in Canada from information in the Office of the Commanding R. Engineer," 1841, *op. cit.*
12. "Report — Toronto — New Barrack Establishment," June 9, 1841, LAC, W.O. 55, Vol. 876. See also "New Barrack Establishment Toronto, as completed" by Captain Vincent Biscoe, R.E., December 2, 1841, LAC, NMC-5394.
13. Notebook and Sketchbook of Thomas Glegg, 1841—1842, Archives of Ontario; Lieutenant Minor Knowlton, "Copy of a Report on

Notes

the Military Establishments of the British Provinces," December 3, 1840, United States Military Academy, Special Collections Archives (transcription by Carl Benn, published in *The York Pioneer*, Vol. 98, 2003. Benn notes that although made of wood, a double thickness stockade such as the one built to enclose the New Fort would have been bulletproof, and probably could have withstood canister and exploding shot, and even some smaller calibre round shot.

14. "Report and Estimate of the probable expense of Various Services proposed to Complete the New Barrack Establishment at Toronto Canada," December 29, 1841, LAC, WO55/877, 357–369.
15. "Report and Estimate of the Probable Expense of Constructing Ball Courts at the Principal Military Stations in Canada," Royal Engineers Office, Montreal, January 13, 1842, LAC, W.O. 55, Vol. 877. "Fives" is a ballgame played with gloved hands or with bats in a court with three or four walls.
16. "Toronto C.W." (detail), by Lieutenant A.R. Vyvyan Crease, R.E., January 1852, LAC, NMC, P/440-Toronto-1852.
17. "Report and Estimate of the Probable Expense of Various Services Proposed to Complete The New Barrack Establishment at Toronto Canada," December 29, 1841, *op. cit.*; Lieutenant-Colonel R. Spark to H. Cornwall, Barrack Office, Toronto, May 17, 1842, LAC, RG8, "C" Series, Vol. 595, 139; Barrack Master H. Cornwall to the Respective Officers, May 18, 1842, LAC, RG8, "C" Series, Vol. 595, 138.
18. Captain R.W. Story, R.A., Vincent Biscoe, R.E., and J.A. Harvey, Department of Ordnance, to the Respective Officer of Ordnance, Toronto, May 23, 1842, LAC, RG8, "C" Series, Vol. 595, 137; Major T. Foster *et al.* to Military Secretary, Headquarters, May 30, 1842, LAC, RG8, C Series, Vol. 595, 141.
19. Diary of Lieutenant Arthur Henry Freeling, R.E., entry for April 13, 1842, LAC, 67/141; James E. Alexander, *Passages in the Life of a Soldier; or, Military Service in the East and West,* Vol. I (London: Hurst and Blackett, 1857), 232.
20. Richard A. Preston, "Military Influence on the Development of Canada," in *The Canadian Military: A Profile,* ed. Hector J. Massey (Canada: Copp Clark, 1972), 60–61.

21. Dr. William Orde Mackenzie's Canadian Diary, entries for April 26, October 4, and October 21, 1839, University of Toronto, Thomas Fisher Rare Book Library, Mss. 5274.
22. Diary of Lieutenant Arthur Henry Freeling, *op cit.*
23. Preston, *op. cit.*, 60.
24. Dr. William Orde Mackenzie's Canadian Diary, *op. cit.*, entry for September 2, 1839.
25. Gilbert Elliot to Lady Minto, October 8, 1847, National Library of Scotland (hereafter cited as NLS), Letters of Gilbert Elliot, MS. 11901.
26. Gilbert Elliot to Lady Harriet Elliot, December 14, 1847, NLS, Letters of Gilbert Elliot, MS. 11782; Gilbert Elliot to Lady Charlotte Elliot, June 16, 1848, NLS, Letters of Gilbert Elliot, MS. 11764. "Tea fight" is a late-1840s term for "tea party."
27. Gilbert Elliot to Lady Harriet Elliot, August 7, September 22 and September 24, 1847, NLS, Letters of Gilbert Elliot, MS. 11782.
28. Gilbert Elliot to Lady Minto, January 28, 1848, NLS, Letters of Gilbert Elliot, MS. 11901; Gilbert Elliot to Lady Harriet Elliot, December 14, 1847, MS. 11782.
29. Gilbert Elliot to Lady Harriet Elliot, August 18, 1848, NLS, Letters of Gilbert Elliot, MS. 11764.
30. Gilbert Elliot to Lady Minto, January 10, 1849, and January 28, 1848, NLS, Letters of Gilbert Elliot, MS. 11901.
31. Gilbert Elliot to Lady Harriet Elliot, August 18, 1848, NLS, Letters of Gilbert Elliot, MS. 11764; Gilbert Elliot to Lady Minto, April 4, 1849, NLS, Letters of Gilbert Elliot, MS. 11901.
32. Gilbert Elliot to Lady Charlotte Elliot, December 22, 1848, NLS, Letters of Gilbert Elliot, MS. 11764; Journal of Gilbert Elliot, entry for March 21, 1850, NLS, MS. 11764; Journal of Gilbert Elliot, entries for April 27, 1850 and November 20, 1850, NLS, MS. 12016.
33. Gilbert Elliot to Lady Harriet Elliot, February 27, 1848, NLS, Letters of Gilbert Elliot, MS.11764; Gilbert to Lady Charlotte Elliot, April 20, 1849, NLS, Letters of Gilbert Elliot, MS. 11783.
34. Gilbert Elliot to Lady Minto, May 4, 1849, NLS, Letters of Gilbert Elliot, MS. 11901.
35. Journal of the Chief Constable 1851–1852, entry for July 23, 1851,

Notes

City of Toronto Archives (hereafter cited as CTA), Municipal Records, Section A, York County, Toronto; Journal of the High Bailiff 1849–1851, entry for June 8, 1849, CTA, Municipal Records, Section A, York County, Toronto. The following are some examples of arrests reported in the Garrison Common area: "… proceeded this morning about four o Clock to the Commons above the New Lunatic Asylum in search of some disorderly characters. Succeeded in arresting Eight — six women and two men." (Journal of the High Bailiff, entry for June 14, 1849.) Proceeded "to the Garrison Commons, where we succeeded in arresting *nine* disorderly females." (Journal of the Chief Constable, entry for August 3, 1850.) "[W]ent to the Garrison Commons, but succeeded in arresting only two disorderly characters." (Journal of the Chief Constable, entry for August 25, 1850.) Constable on duty "reported the arrest of four women (disorderly females) from the Garrison Commons." (Journal of the Chief Constable, October 6, 1851.)

36. City Council Minutes, Toronto, May 20, 1850, CTA, (#303).
37. Report by A. Mackenzie Fraser, deputy quartermaster general's office, Montreal, June 26, 1847, LAC, RG8, "C" Series, Vol. 31, 85–86.
38. Stacey, *op cit.,* 23.
39. George T. Denison, *Soldiering in Canada: Recollections and Experiences* 2nd ed., (Toronto: George N. Morang and Company Limited, 1901), 30.
40. "Canada, Toronto, Plan shewing the Boundaries as marked on the ground of the Military Reserve belonging to the Ordnance in the City of Toronto, County and Township of York, Canada West, as Surveyed by Mr. Sandford Fleming, Provincial Land Surveyor, between the months of Novr. 1851 & May 1852," LAC, 11449, (R) H1/440/Toronto/1852; William H. Boulton to Sir Richard Jackson, Commander of the Forces, January 24, 1845, LAC, RG8, "C" Series, Vol. 519, 216–18; William F. Coffin, commissioner of ordnance and admiralty lands, to E.A. Meredith, deputy of the minister of the interior, July 13, 1874, LAC, RG9, IIA1, Vol. 64, File 9994.
41. John Withrow, "Born Out of Protest," in *Once Upon a Century: 100 Year History of the "Ex"* (Toronto: J.H. Robinson Publishing Limited, 1978), 13.

42. See, for example, "The Defence of Canada," in *Blackwood's Edinburgh Magazine*, Vol. XCI, No. DLVI, February 1862, 228–258.
43. By the 1880s, the Old Fort would be declared obsolete by the Canadian military. However, it continued to be used as an auxiliary facility to the New Fort, mainly as storage space and as married quarters, until the 1930s, when the Old Fort became a museum. Benn, "Toronto's Forgotten Fort," *op. cit.*
44. W. Howard Russell, *Canada: Its Defences, Condition, and Resources, Being a Second and Concluding Volume of "My Diary, North and South"* 2nd ed. (Boston: T.O.H.P. Burnham, 1865), 5, 55, 209.
45. "Inscriptions of tablets outside main grouping," Strachan Avenue Cemetery, FYA; John Ross Robertson, *Robertson's Landmarks of Toronto: A Collection of Historical Sketches of the Old Town of York from 1792 until 1833, and of Toronto from 1834 to 1893*, Vol. I (Toronto: J. Ross Robertson, 1894), 67.
46. W. Edwards, Secretary, Electoral Division Society, to Sir George E. Cartier, minister of militia, September 1, 1869, LAC, RG9, IIA1, Vol. 12, File 1849.
47. "A Month's Leave, or, The Cruise of the *Breeze*" (Diary of Harry E. Baines), Chapter Two, Prince Edward County Archives.
48. Skittles is a game resembling bowling.
49. V.M. Roberts, "The Garrison Reserve," in Roberts, "Memorabilia — Being a Collection of Extracts Relating to the Origin of the Name Toronto, and the History of the Water Front of the City, its Harbour and Shipping, from 1669 to 1912. Gathered from Standard Authorities and Newspapers," (Vol. V), 3, Toronto Harbour Commission Archives; "Relative Sketch Shewing the Position of the Batteries," LAC, NMC, H4/440-Toronto-1868-No. 1; "Report on the Canada Barracks Visited and Inspected in Oct. 1863 by Lt.-Col. Jervois and Capt. R. Harrison," LAC, RG8, Series II, Vol. 34, 47, 102–107.
50. Francis Duncan, *Our Garrisons in the West or Sketches in British North America* (London: Chapman and Hall, 1864), 201; Russell, *op. cit.*, 51.
51. See, for example, "City News", in the *Evening Globe*, January 4, 1870, 1.
52. Desmond Morton, *The Canadian General: Sir William Otter* (Toronto:

Hakkert, 1974), 17; George F.G. Stanley, "Military Education in Canada, 1867–1970", in Massey, *op. cit.*, 170.

53. "Annual Report of the Detachment 1st Battalion 60th Royal Rifles stationed at Toronto," LAC, McGrigor Papers, MG 40, F1 Vol. 2.
54. George F.G. Stanley, *Toil and Trouble: Military Expeditions to Red River* (Canadian War Museum Publication No. 25), (Toronto: Dundurn, 1989), 250; "Red River Expedition," *The Daily Globe*, May 11, 1870, 3.
55. Memo, Department of Militia and Defence, June 25, 1870, LAC, RG9, IIA1, Vol. 21, File 3399.
56. Report from Lieutenant-Colonel Thomas Wily to the minister of militia and defence, July 21, 1870, LAC, RG9, IIA1, Vol. 21, File 3432.
57. Lieutenant-Colonel Thomas Wily to the minister of militia and defence, September 30, 1870, LAC, RG9, IIA1, File 3432.

CHAPTER TWO: THE CANADIAN PERIOD (1870–1914)

1. Sam B. Steele, *Forty Years in Canada: Reminiscences of the Great North-West with Some Account of his Service in South Africa* (New York: Dodd, Mead and Company, 1915), 49–50. Steele notes with admiration that Goodwin, who had served at Waterloo under the Duke of Wellington in 1815, was still in excellent physical form.
2. C.S. Gzowski to Sir George E. Cartier, minister of militia and defence, Ottawa, August 27, 1870, and P. Robertson-Ross to minister of militia and defence, September 3, 1870, LAC, RG9, IIA1, Vol. 23, File 3786.
3. C.S. Gzowski to Robert B. Denison, August 10, 1872, and Robert B. Denison, acting deputy adjutant general to the deputy adjutant general of militia, Ottawa, August 13, 1872, LAC, RG9, IIA1, Vol. 43, File 6952; Memo from Lieutenant-Colonel Thomas Wily, director of stores, August 1, 1871, LAC, RG9, IIA1, Vol. 32, File 3204.
4. Major D. Irwin, Kingston, to Lieutenant-Colonel Powell, acting adjutant general, Ottawa, February 10, 1874, LAC, RG9, IIA1, Vol. 59, File 9203; Lieutenant-Colonel Goodwin to Lieutenant-Colonel Thomas Wily, February 16, 1874, LAC, RG9, IIA1, Vol. 59, File 9226.

5. In October of 1871, the Canadian government had been forced by the withdrawal of the British to form two small units of garrison artillery, to take charge of the stores left in Canada by the British. These units, designated "A" and "B" Batteries, garrisoned the forts at Quebec and Kingston, and provided gunnery schools for the militia.
6. Report from Lieutenant-Colonel Durie, deputy adjutant general, Military District No. 2, Old Fort, Toronto, to the acting adjutant general of Militia, Headquarters, Ottawa, March 4, 1874, LAC, RG9, IIA1, Vol. 59, File 9226.
7. Report from Lieutenant-Colonel Durie, *ibid.*; Sergeant George A. Crush, Old Fort, March 24, 1874 to Lieutenant-Colonel Goodwin, Military Storekeeper, Toronto; and Lieutenant-Colonel Goodwin to Lieutenant-Colonel Wily, Mary 24, 1874, LAC, RG9, IIA1, Vol. 59, File 9226.
8. Telegram, T.A. Scoble to Lieutenant-Colonel Wily, February 16, 1874; Lieutenant-Colonel Thomas A. Scoble, Toronto, to Lieutenant-Colonel Wily, director of stores, Ottawa, March 13, 1874; Memo from Lieutenant-Colonel Wily, March 16, 1874; and Memo, Lieutenant-Colonel Thomas Wily, April 17, 1874, LAC, RG9, IIA1, Vol. 59, File 9226.
9. Nora and William Kelly, *The Royal Canadian Mounted Police: A Century of History 1873–1973* (Edmonton: Hurtig, 1973), 13; S.W. Horall, "The March West," in Hugh A. Dempsey, *Men in Scarlet* (Calgary: Historical Society of Alberta/McClelland & Stewart West, n.d.), 16; C.W. Harvison, "Preface," in Harvison, *The Horsemen* (Toronto and Montreal: McClelland & Stewart), xii–xiii.
10. John A. Macdonald as quoted in S.W. Horall, "Sir John A. Macdonald and the Mounted Police Force for the Northwest Territories," in *Canadian Historical Review,* LIII, 1972, 181; Harvison, *op. cit.,* xiv. The Royal Irish Constabulary served as the model upon which colonial police forces were patterned throughout the British Empire in the nineteenth century. The Constabulary fulfilled the judicial functions of police officers while also having the military capabilities of an armed force.
11. Ronald Atkin, *Maintain the Right: The Early History of the North West*

Mounted Police, 1873–1900 (Toronto: Macmillan, 1973), 40; Kelly, *op. cit.,* 16. Although the force was commonly called "N.W.M.P." from its earliest days, this was not the official name of the force until the May 23, 1873, act was amended in 1879. See Jim Wallace, *A Double Duty: The Decisive First Decade of the North West Mounted Police* (Winnipeg: Bunker to Bunker Books, 1997), 19.

12. Kelly, *op. cit.,* 17.
13. Atkin, *op. cit.,* 44; Wallace, *op. cit.,* 28.
14. P. Robertson-Ross as quoted in R.G. MacBeth, *Policing the Plains, Being the Real-Life Record of the Famous North-West Mounted Police* (London: Hodder and Staughton, 1922), 25.
15. As described by Captain Cecil E. Denny, who joined the N.W.M.P. with a commission in the spring of 1874. Cecil E. Denny, *The Riders of The Plains: A Reminiscence of the Early and Exciting Days in the North West* (Calgary: The Herald Company, Limited, 1905), 18; Cecil E. Denny, *The Law Marches West,* ed. W.B. Cameron (Toronto: J.M. Dent and Sons, 1972), 10.
16. William Parker to his father, April 21, 1874, Glenbow Museum Archives (hereafter cited as GMA), William Parker Papers, M934, File 6.
17. Denny, *The Riders of The Plains, op. cit.*; Michael Craufurd-Lewis, *Macleod of the Mounties: The North American Saga as seen through the life of a Scottish Canadian Hero* (Ottawa, The Golden Dog Press, 1999), 135.
18. Philip Goldring, "The First Contingent: The North-West Mounted Police, 1873–74," in *Canadian Historic Sites: Occasional Papers in Archaeology and History No. 21* (Ottawa: Parks Canada, 1979), 13–14; Atkin, *op. cit.,* 46; Steele, *op. cit.,* 52–53.
19. Atkin, *op.cit.,* 42, 46–48; Wallace, *op. cit.,* 37.
20. Craufurd-Lewis, *op. cit.,* 147; S.W. Horrall, *The Pictorial History of the Royal Canadian Mounted Police* (Toronto: McGraw-Hill Ryerson Limited, 1973), 42; Atkin, *op. cit.,* 50.
21. Jean d'Artigue, *Six Years in the Canadian North-West* (Toronto: Hunter, Rose and Company, 1882), 11–13.
22. D'Artigue, *ibid.,* 14.
23. Atkin, *op.cit.,* 50–51.

24. Fred A. Bagley, *The '74 Mounties* (unpublished manuscript), 1938, GMA, Fred A. Bagley Papers, M43, Ch. II, 6. Bagley is referring to a popular Irish song of the period, "Father O'Flynn."
25. William Parker, "Thirty Eight and a Half Years Service and Experience in the Mounties" (unpublished manuscript), n.d., GMA, William Parker Papers, M934, File 22, Ch. II.
26. Denny, *The Law Marches West, op. cit.,* 9; Bagley, *The '74 Mounties, op. cit.*
27. Ernest J. Chambers, *The Royal North-West Mounted Police: A Corps History* (Montreal and Ottawa: Mortimer Press, 1906), 21; R.C. Macleod, *The N.W.M.P. and Law Enforcement 1873–1905* (Toronto: University of Toronto Press, 1976), 112.
28. Macleod, *ibid.,* 74, 86. Interestingly, Sergeant-Major Sam Steele was frustrated by the lack of what he considered to be effective punishments for the men, who were, he said, not "plaster saints," but human beings with human weaknesses: "… it was not until two years later that the officers were given proper disciplinary powers over the force, which in every respect had more the characteristics of a first-class cavalry regiment than those of an ordinary rural police," Steele, *op cit.,* 61.
29. William Parker to his mother, April 5, 1874, reprinted in Hugh A. Dempsey, *William Parker: Mounted Policeman* (Edmonton: Hurtig, 1973), 101.
30. William Parker, "Thirty-Eight and a Half Years Service," *op. cit.*; William Parker to his mother, April 5, 1874, reprinted in Dempsey, *op. cit.,* 101–02.
31. William Parker to his father, April 15, 1874, GMA, William Parker Papers, M934, File 6.
32. William Parker to his father, April 21, 1874, GMA, William Parker Papers, M934, File 6.
33. Diary of William Parker 1874, entry for April 10, 1874, GMA, William Parker Papers, M934, File 1; D'Artigue, *op. cit.,* 16.
34. Atkin, *op. cit.,* 50; Wallace, *op. cit.,* 38.
35. Fred A. Bagley as quoted in Macleod, *op cit.,* 85; Bagley, *The '74 Mounties, op cit.,* Ch. II, 7–8.

Notes

36. Major General P. Selby Smyth to minister of militia and defence, March 10, 1875, LAC, RG9, IIA1, Vol. 71, File 01270; Colonel Thomas Scoble to Lieutenant-Colonel Wily, director of stores, April 28, 1874, LAC, RG9, IIA1, Vol. 59, File 9226.
37. Parker, "Thirty-Eight and a Half Years Service," *op. cit.*; Bagley, *The '74 Mounties, op cit.*, Ch. II, 6–7.
38. D'Artigue, *op. cit.*, 16–17.
39. William Parker to his father, June 3, 1874, reprinted in Dempsey, 103.
40. Denny, *The Riders of The Plains, op. cit.*, 23; A.L. Haydon, *The Riders of the Plains: A Record of the Royal North-West Mounted Police of Canada, 1873-1910* (Edmonton: Hurtig, 1971), 22; D'Artigue, *op. cit.*, 17–18.
41. D'Artigue, *ibid.*, 19. Cecil Denny recalled that, "We were from the start to the finish the objects of the greatest interest to the public, being surrounded from morning to night with crowds of people, ever ready to assist us. There was nothing they would not and did not do for us." Denny, *The Riders of The Plains, op. cit.*, 24.
42. D'Artigue, *op. cit.*, 119–20.
43. Atkin, *op. cit.*, 51.
44. D'Artigue, *op. cit.*, 20; Kelly, *op. cit.*, 25; Atkin, *op. cit.*, 51.
45. D'Artigue, *ibid.*
46. William F. Coffin to E.A. Meredith, Department of the minister of the interior, July 13, 1874, and Lieutenant-Colonel W. Powell, acting adjutant general of militia, to minister of militia and Defence, August 7, 1874, LAC, RG9, IIA1, Vol. 64, File 9994. The map on page 68 shows the changing size of the military reserve over the years.
47. Major-General E. Selby-Smyth, general officer commanding, to the minister of militia and defence, March 10, 1875, LAC, RG9, IIA1, Vol. 71, File 01270.
48. Withrow, *op. cit.*, 14–17; Order in Council (Privy Council), March 1, 1899, LAC, RG9, IIA1, Vol. 314, File 17420 ½; Lieutenant-Colonel W.D. Otter to the minister of militia and defence, March 13, 1878, LAC, RG9, IIA1, Vol. 88, File 04291.
49. Telegram, William Durie to Colonel Powell, September 8, 1879, LAC, RG9, IIA1, Vol. 99, File 05922.

50. Memo from Major-General E. Selby-Smyth, April 13, 1880, LAC, RG9, IIA1, Vol. 103, File 06415.
51. Ontario Rifle Association Lease, 1881, LAC, RG9, IIA1, Vol. 124, File 08902; W.D. Otter to Lieutenant-Colonel Panet, deputy of the minister of militia, December 16, 1881, LAC, RG9 IIA1, Vol. 118, File 08188.
52. Stephen J. Harris, *Canadian Brass: The Making of a Professional Army, 1860–1939* (Toronto: University of Toronto Press, 1988), 17–18; George F.G. Stanley, *Canada's Soldiers 1604–1954: The Military History of an Unmilitary People* (Toronto: Macmillan, 1954), 248.
53. Morton, *op. cit.,* 92; Toronto *Globe,* November 28, 1883, as quoted in Roberts, *op. cit.,* 22.
54. "Col. Otter's Command: A Visit to the Canadian Regulars at the New Fort" Toronto *Globe,* April 11, 1884, 5.
55. "Col. Otter's Command," *ibid.*; "Plan of Buildings used as Officer's Quarters, New Fort Barracks, Toronto," 1889, LAC, C-6847.
56. "Plan of Buildings used as Officer's Quarters, New Fort Barracks, Toronto," 1889, *ibid.*; "Col. Otter's Command," *op. cit.,* 5.
57. "Canada's Grand Old Military Man, As Related by Sir William Otter to a Staff Writer of The *Sunday World,*" Toronto *Sunday World,* Magazine Section, 25, December 30, 1923, Canadian War Museum (hereafter cited as CWM), 58A1, 102, Otter Fonds.
58. R.C. Fetherstonhaugh, *The Royal Canadian Regiment 1883–1933* (Canada: The Royal Canadian Regiment, 1936), 13; "Military Inspection," Toronto *Mail,* July 30, 1884, 8; "Valiant Canadian Soldier Answers Last Call," Toronto *Evening Telegram,* May 7, 1929, CWM, 58A1, 102, Otter Fonds.
59. Molly Otter to Adolphe Caron, August 21, 1888, in Morton, *op. cit.,* 134; Harris, *op. cit.,* 26.
60. Correspondence, The general officer commanding, re: "That the sanitary condition of the New Fort Barracks and of the buildings at the Old Fort, Toronto, is most unsatisfactory," August 30, October 6, December 19, December 26, and December 28, 1892, LAC, RG9, IIA1, Vol. 263, File A12272.
61. Harris, *op. cit.,* 26.

62. Similarly, protests against the establishment of the Royal Military College in 1874 had been assuaged by assurances that its graduates, like those of the United States Military Academy at West Point, would be trained to be useful in civilian, as well as military, life. Stanley, "Military Education," *op. cit.,* 172.
63. Dom Pedro, "Old Times at the New Fort," in Pedro, *Sketches* (Toronto: self-published, 1891), 29.
64. Fetherstonhaugh, *op. cit.,* 22; Morton, *op. cit.,* 130–31; "Illuminated Address from the City of Toronto, March 1885," LAC, MG30, E242.
65. John Slatter, president, Toronto Orchestral Association, to Adolphe Caron, minister of militia and defence, October 2, 1891, LAC, RG9, IIA1, Vol. 254, File A11436.
66. Pedro, *op. cit.,* 11.
67. "Proceedings of a Court of Inquiry assembled at New Fort Barracks, Toronto on the 13th September 1887," LAC, RG9, IIA1, Vol. 205, File A7124.
68. James Hamilton to Adolphe Caron, March 12, 1888, LAC, RG9, IIA1, Vol. 211, File A7712.
69. Pedro, *op. cit.,* 11–12.
70. L.H. Baldwin to W.D. Otter, June 25, 1888, LAC, RG9, IIA1, Vol. 211, File A7712; Captain J.B. McLean, Royal Grenadiers, to Lieutenant-Colonel George B. Dawson, Commanding Royal Grenadiers, June 27, 1888, LAC, RG9, IIA1, Vol. 211, File A7712; Otter to Powell, June 30, 1888, LAC, RG9, IIA1, Vol. 211, File A7712.
71. John Shaw, mayor of Toronto, to Dr. Borden, minister of militia, September 23, 1897, LAC, RG9, IIA1, Vol. 302, File 16187.
72. In 1887, a fourth ("D") company of infantry had been authorized for London, Ontario.
73. Fetherstonhaugh, *op. cit.,* 44. In 1899, the name of the regiment was changed to the "Royal Canadian Regiment of Infantry."
74. Stanley, *Canada's Soldiers, op. cit.,* 266.
75. Lord Stanley, who served as Canada's sixth governor general, is probably best remembered for his donation in 1892 of a trophy for the amateur hockey championship in Canada. The "Dominion Hockey Challenge Cup" soon became known as the "Stanley Cup." See Kevin

Shea and John Jason Wilson, *Lord Stanley: The Man Behind the Cup* (Bolton, ON: H.B. Fenn and Company, 2006).

76. Brereton Greenhous, *Dragoon* (Belleville, ON: Guild of the Royal Canadian Dragoons, 1983), 42–43.
77. Fetherstonhaugh, *op. cit.,* 65–66.
78. Fetherstonhaugh, *ibid.,* 86–87.
79. Upon his return to Toronto from the South African campaign, Otter was reappointed to the command of Military District No. 2, but was no longer in command of the infantry school. He and Molly moved from Stanley Barracks to a house on Beverly Street. Morton, *op. cit.,* 245, 258.
80. Clara Ellen Worthington, *"The Spur and the Sprocket": The Story of the Royal Canadian Dragoons* (CFB Gagetown, NB: Royal Canadian Dragoons, 1968), 14.
81. Greenhous, *op. cit.,* 75, 77.
82. Interview with Mrs. Carol Snell (Steer's granddaughter), February 23, 1990.
83. "Bugler Daniel P. Stevens," the Aurora *Banner*, January 11, 1901 (clipping from the collection of the Aurora Museum), FYA, "Stanley Barracks — General" File.
84. Greenhous, *op. cit.,* 76; Fetherstonhaugh, *op. cit.,* 162; Morton, *op. cit.,* 247.
85. Commanding Officer, No. 2 R.D., Royal Canadian Regiment, Stanley Barracks, Toronto, to deputy officer commanding, Military District No. 2, February 16, 1900, LAC, RG9, IIA1, Vol. 327, File 18729.
86. F.L. Lessard to deputy officer commanding, Military District No. 2, October 18, 1899, LAC, RG9, IIA1, Vol. 319, File 17888. The "Victoria Cross dummy" referred to was most likely a prop from a popular military sporting tradition of the time known as a "Victoria Cross Race." In this event, participants, mounted on horses, raced to pick up a straw-filled dummy representing a wounded soldier, and carry it back to "safety" (i.e., the finish line), usually jumping hurdles along the way.
87. Morton, *op. cit.,* 252; W.J. Bailey and E.R. Toop, *Canadian Military Post Offices to 1986* (Toronto: Unitrade Press, 1987), 3.
88. Worthington, *op. cit.,* 39–41.

Notes

89. Gerald Killan, *Preserving Ontario's Past* (Ottawa: Love Printing Service Limited, 1976), 137–38.
90. "Move Stanley Barracks," Toronto *Globe,* September 11, 1901, 9; Sir Frederick Borden, minister of militia and defence, to Mr. R.J. Fleming, assessment commissioner, October 19, 1903, in V.M. Roberts, "The Old Fort," *Memorabilia,* 1904–1934, Vol. 16, 24.
91. General Otter to Major J.W. Thomas, Secretary, OFPA, March 7, 1908, MTPL, Baldwin Room, Old Fort Protective Association (OFPA) Papers.
92. Wilfrid Laurier to J.O. Thorn, March 30, 1909, MTPL, Baldwin Room, OFPA Papers; Killan, *op. cit.,* 160–61.
93. James Wilson, commissioner of parks to the mayor (chairman) and members, Board of Control, September 22, 1908, CTA, Department of Parks and Recreation (hereafter cited as DPR), RG12, A, Box 6; Attachment to Memo from DPR to Chambers, CTA, Fonds 200, Series 487, File 477; James Wilson to Brigadier-General Otter, O.C. Western Command, September 21, 1908, CTA, DPR, RG12, A, Box 6.
94. Interviews with Mrs. Lois Campbell, daughter of Colour Sergeant William Charles Carter, April 26 and 27, 1989; Mrs. Doris E. Collins to author, May 7, 1989; interview with Mrs. Weller, neighbourhood resident 1910–1913, June 19, 1989.
95. "Hard at work in camp at Levis," Toronto *Globe,* August 16, 1910, 16; "Official Approval Tour of Queen's Own," Toronto *Globe,* August 10, 1910, 9.
96. Greenhous, *op. cit.,* 164.

CHAPTER THREE: THE WORLD WARS (1914–1945)

1. William A. Craick, "Notes from Toronto Newspapers," Vol. 27, referencing the Toronto *Mail and Empire,* August 7 and 26, 1913, and November 22, 1913, and the Toronto *Globe,* July 4, 1914, MTPL, Baldwin Room; and C.N.E., "Official Catalogue and Programme, C.N.E., 1914," C.N.E. Archives.

2. "Rain Tests Mettle of Exhibition Crowd," Toronto *Globe,* September 2, 1914, 1.
3. Craick, *op. cit.,* Vol. 28, referencing the Toronto *Globe,* September 19, 1914.
4. C.N.E. Association, "Report of the Thirty-Sixth Annual Meeting held at the City Hall, Toronto," 1914, 43–46, C.N.E. Archives.
5. A.D. Camp and L.F. Atkins, *7th Toronto Regiment, Royal Regiment of Canadian Artillery 1866-1966* (Toronto: 7th Toronto Regiment, RCA, nd.), 9.
6. J.E. Middleton, "Canadian War Camps," in *Canada in the Great War* by Various Authorities, Vol. II (Toronto: United Publishers of Canada Limited, 1919), 253; "March of Tingling Troops Like Mammoth Snow Plough," Toronto *Globe,* December 23, 1914, 5.
7. Middleton, *op. cit.*; Percival J. Lee, Area Supervisor, Y.M.C.A., to Major-General W.A. Logie, officer commanding. Military District No. 2, November 16, 1917, LAC, RG24, Vol. 4349, 34-5-12; "Home Guards are Now Militia Regiment," Toronto *Globe,* December 24, 1914, 7.
8. J. Castell Hopkins, *The Canadian Annual Review of Public Affairs: 1914* (Toronto: Annual Review Publishing Company, 1915), 336; Middleton, *op. cit.,* 253. Also Barbara M. Wilson, "Introduction," in *Ontario and the First World War 1914–1918: A Collection of Documents,* ed., Wilson (Toronto: University of Toronto Press, 1977), cvi, xl.
9. Middleton, *op. cit.,* 255; "Great Host of Features Planned for Big Fair," Toronto *Globe,* August 28, 1915, 7; Wilson, *op. cit.,* xxxiv.
10. Wilson, *ibid.,* xxviii; Memo to Officer in care of Troops, Exhibition Camp, 29 January 1919, LAC, RG24, Vol. 4354, 43-5-44, Vol. 1.
11. Memo, April 5, 1918, LAC, RG24, Vol. 4353, 34-5-44, Vol. 1; Memo, May 3, 1918, LAC, RG24, Vol. 4353, 34-5-44, Vol. 1.
12. Hopkins, *op. cit.,* 336; Craick, *op. cit.,* Vol. 28, referencing the Toronto *Globe,* December 2, 1914.
13. C.N.E., "Official Catalogue and Program, C.N.E., 1916," and "Official Catalogue and Program, C.N.E., 1917," C.N.E. Archives.
14. "A Soldier" to Brigadier-General Gunn, general officer commanding, Military District No. 2, February 9, 1919, LAC, RG24, Vol. 4353, 34-5-44, Vol. 2; Inspection Report by Lieutenant F.C. Hemtzman,

Camp Field Officer of the Day, LAC, RG24, Vol. 4354, 34-5-44, Vol. 1.

15. Anonymous to the prime minister, April 2, 1918, LAC, RG24, Vol. 2023, File HQC-965, 193–97. Presumably, the "German wife" in Russia referred to is Tsarina Alexandra, the German-born wife of Tsar Nicholas II, who was highly unpopular during the war with the Russian people due to numerous, but unfounded, rumours that she was collaborating with the German government.

16. Letters received by the government or the police reporting "suspicious" neighbours were investigated by the Royal North-West Mounted Police, and in many cases the persons in question were found to be respectable, patriotic citizens. Others were interned, and R.N.W.M.P. files reveal the reasoning behind the decisions to intern certain individuals. Here are two examples: "Arrested at Empress, Alberta, on account of having expressed pro-German sentiments. This man has been to the U.S.A. and back without permission, and is an active member of the I.W.W.'s [the Industrial Workers of the World labour union]. Is considered to be dangerous at large." And: "Is of fit age for a soldier and has been causing trouble amongst the aliens at the Manitoba and Saskatchewan Mine. Has been talking pro-German and assaulted a Russian because the Russian's brother joined a Canadian Overseas Battalion." A report on a twenty-two-year-old in Lethbridge, Alberta, who had emigrated from Germany in April 1914 stated: "He has expressed strong pro-German sentiments and is in possession of seditious writing. Has also been conducting correspondence with German soldiers on active duty." The German soldiers turned out to be the man's cousin and brother. The R.N.W.M.P. officer investigating the case, finding insufficient evidence to prosecute, reported "so, for safety sake, I am ordering this man's detention in the Internment Camp." He was interned at Banff. "Schedule of POW handed over to the Department of Militia by the RNWM Police for Internment," May 1917, LAC, RG18, Vol. 519, File RCMP 1917, Nos. 10 Part I.

17. Morton, *op. cit.,* 328–29; Circular letter, adjutant general, Canadian militia to general officer commanding, 2nd Division, November 21, 1914, LAC, RG24, Vol. .4287, 34-1-26, Vol. 1; Craick, *op. cit.,* Vol. 28,

referencing the Toronto *Globe,* December 18, 1914, and December 22, 1914; Joseph A. Boudreau, "The Enemy Alien Problem in Canada, 1914-1921" (unpublished Ph.D. diss., UCLA, 1965), p. 34; Major-General Sir William Otter, "Report on Internment Operations, Canada, 1914–1920," (Ottawa, 1921), reprinted as Appendix A in Lubomyr Luciuk, *In Fear of the Barbed Wire Fence: Canada's First National Internment Operations and the Ukrainian Canadians, 1914–1920* (Kingston: Kashtan Press, 2001). Accommodations for women and children internees was only available at the Spirit Lake, Quebec and Vernon, B.C. camps.

18. Morton, *op. cit.,* 329; Robert H. Coats, "The Alien Enemy in Canada: Internment Operations," in *Canada in the Great War, op. cit.,* 154–55; "How Canada Handled Her Prisoners of War, as related by Sir William Otter to a Staff Writer of the Sunday *World*," Toronto *Daily World,* January 27, 1924, CWM, 58A1, 102.4a, General Otter Fonds; Otter, "Report on Internment Operations," *op. cit.*

19. Memo, general officer commanding, 2nd Division to Secretary, Military Council, August 24, 1914, LAC, RG24, Vol. 4276, 34-1-3, Vol. 1; Memo, general officer commanding to Secretary, Military Council, September 8, 1914, LAC, RG24, Vol. 4276, 34-1-3, Vol. 1; Memo, September 7, 1914, LAC, RG24, Vol. 4276, 34-1-3, Vol. 1.

20. Report re: Stanley Barracks Internment Station, officer commanding, Military District No. 2, to Otter, December 16, 1914, LAC, RG24, Vol. 4287, 34-1-26, Vol. 1; "Floor Plan of Subdivided Buildings, Stanley Barracks, Toronto," by Major Lawrence Buchan, RRCI, January 19, 1894, LAC, NMC, C-49451; "Stanley Barracks, Toronto," by Lieutenant H.J. Burden, 9th M.H., May 7, 1915, FYA, 1989.31.35.b.

21. Report re Prisoners at Stanley Barracks, October 15, 1914, LAC, RG24, Vol. 4276, 34-1-3, Vol. 2; GOC, 2nd Division to Otter, December 17, 1914, LAC, RG24, Vol. 4276, 34-1-3, Vol.4.

22. LAC, RG24, Vol. 4278, 34-1-3, Vol.8; RG24, Vol. 4279, 34-1-3, Vol. 9.

23. Morton, *op. cit.,* 330; Report re Stanley Barracks Internment Station, *op. cit.*

24. Major-General Sir Willliam Otter, "Report on Internment Operations," *op. cit.*; William D. Otter Diaries, CWM, 58A1, 102.1,

Notes

19910162-154-161. Upon the death of Otter in 1929, his friends would reflect on his outstanding administrative skills and attention to detail: "Sir William was a most painstaking man," noted Sir Henry Pellatt, who had served with Otter in the Queen's Own Rifles. Colonel Henry Brock, also formerly of the Queen's Own, added, "Sir William was a very hard worker and a splendid bookkeeper." "Valiant Canadian Soldier Answers Last Call," Toronto *Evening Telegram*, May 7, 1929, CWM, 58A1, 102, Otter Fonds.

25. "How Canada Handled Her Prisoners of War," *op. cit.*; Report re: Stanley Barracks Internment Station, *op. cit.*; Desmond Morton, "Sir William Otter and Internment Operations in Canada during the First World War," *Canadian Historical Review*, Vol. LV, No. 1 (March 1974): 43.

26. Lieutenant-Colonel Elliott to Captain R.S. Wilson, 48th Highlanders, February 9, 1915, and Paul Bimburg to Lieutenant-Colonel Elliott, Feburary 6, 1915, LAC, RG24, Vol 4276, 34-1-3, Vol. 5.

27. Proceeding of Board of Inquiry into Death of #537 Yousseff Hussein, held at Stanley Barracks, April 1, 1916, LAC, RG24, Vol. 4279, 34-1-3, Vol. 11.

28. Otter, "Internment Operations," *op. cit.*; Luciuk, *op. cit.*, p. 44.

29. Memo to Mr. Bradshaw, re: Garrison Common and Old Fort Property, September 24, 1918, CTA, Fonds 200, Series 487, File 217; T. Bradshaw, commissioner of finance and city treasurer, to C.E. Chambers, May 13, 1919, CTA, Fonds 200, Series 487, File 217. The municipal assessment commissioner determined that the rental rate should be $8,413.20 per annum, basing his calculation on a value of $12,000 per acre for the fifteen-and-a-half acres that Stanley Barracks occupied, at 4.5 percent. He also recommended that rent not be charged until the end of the year, at the request of the Department of Militia and Defence, who hoped to have a decision regarding the acquisition of other barracks and stores property by then. Attachment to Memo from DPR to Chambers, *op. cit.*; W.A. Littlejohn to Chambers, May 28, 1920, CTA, Fonds 200, Series 487, File 217; commissioner of parks to mayor and Board of Control, July 9, 1920, CTA, Fonds 200, Series 487, File 217.

30. Memo, Mr. Love to Mr. Chambers, May 29, 1940, CTA, DPR, RG12, A, Box 45, File 3.
31. Greenhous, *op. cit.*, 244; Fetherstonhaugh, *op. cit.*, 392; Ed Johnson, RCD, to author, August 1, 1989; interview with Mrs. Mary Maxted, Fort York resident 1921-1929, February 3, 1988.
32. Dorothy Caroline Steer Brasier, "Stanley Barracks, Toronto, Ont. – Memories," (unpublished account) May 25, 1985, FYA, "Stanley Barracks — General" File; Timmis Diaries, MTPL, Baldwin Room, Reginald Symonds Timmis Fonds, S249.
33. "The Canadian Military International Horse Show Team, 1927, by 'Eye Witness,'" *Canadian Defence Quarterly,* Vol. V (October 1927–July 1928): 230–31; Dudley D. Spencer, "Bucephalus," *Pro Patria*, No. 9 (August 1971), available at *www.theroyalcanadianregiment.ca*; Worthington, *op. cit.,* 72; Greenhous, *op. cit.,* 258–60.
34. Greenhous, *ibid.*
35. Timmis diaries, entries for January 2 and 16, 1924, February 20, 1924, January 29, 1924, February 2, 1924, and January 25, MTPL, Baldwin Room, Reginald Symonds Timmis Fonds, S249.
36. R. Munro as quoted in Greenhous, *op. cit.,* 263.
37. Lieutenant-Colonel Gilman to Mr. C.E. Chambers, commissioner of parks, March 27, 1922, CTA, DPR, RG12, A, Box 19, File 5; G.L.P. Grant-Suttie, captain for A.A. and quartermaster general, Military District No. 2, to Chambers, April 10, 1922, CTA, Fonds 200, Series 487, File 217; Gilman to Chambers, March 22, 1922, CTA, Fonds 200, Series 487, File 217; Captain G.L.P. Grant-Suttie to Chambers, April 10, 1922, CTA, Fonds 200, Series 487, File 217.
38. G.J. Desbarats, acting deputy minister, Department of National Defence, to the deputy minister, Department of Justice, Ottawa, May 15, 1923, LAC, RG13, Vol. 278, File 1923-940; E.L. Newcombe to acting deputy minister, Department of National Defence, Ottawa, September 12, 1923, LAC, RG13, Vol. 278, File 1923-940.
39. "Toronto Should Preserve Her Historic Landmarks," Toronto *Evening Telegram*, February 9, 1926, 12; Memo from DPR to Chambers, April 13, 1926, CTA, Fonds 200, Series 487, File 217.
40. H.W. Waters, assistant manager and secretary, C.N.E. Association, to

C.E. Chambers, commissioner of parks, January 19, 1927, CTA, DPR, RG12, A, Box 21, File 6; H.W. Waters to C.E. Chambers, November 8, 1926, CTA, Fonds 200, Series 487, File 217; W.A. Littlejohn, city clerk, to C.E. Chambers, January 12, 1927, CTA, Fonds 200, Series 487, File 217; H.W. Waters to C.E. Chambers, January 19, 1927, CTA, Fonds 200, Series 487, File 217.

41. W.A. Littlejohn, City Clerk, to C.E. Chambers, February 18, 1927, CTA, Fonds 200, Series 487, File 217.
42. Attachment to Memo from DPR to Chambers, *op. cit.*; "Agreement re: Stanley Barracks & Eastern Entrance to Canadian National Exhibition, 27th June 1927, Between His Majesty the King represented by The Hon. The Minister of National Defence of Canada and The Corporation of the City of Toronto," FYA, "Stanley Barracks – General" File; Report, "Occupation of Stanley Barracks by Militia," by C.E. Chambers, February 22, 1927, CTA, Fonds 200, Series 487, File 217.
43. Attachment to Memo from DPR to Chambers, *op. cit.*
44. Ed Johnson to author, August 1, 1989.
45. Lieutenant-Colonel E.H. Shuter, "Veteran's Tales #2 – Toronto: Stanley Barracks in the 1930s," available at *www.theroyalcanadianregiment.ca*.
46. Major G.R. Chetwynd, RCE, to C.E. Chambers, February 10, 1936, CTA, Fonds 200, Series 487, File 476; Chetwynd to C.E. Chambers, June 9, 1938, CTA, DPR, RG12, Series A, Box 45, File 2.
47. Lieutenant-Colonel E.L. Caldwell, commanding, Stanley Barracks, to C.E. Chambers, April 27, 1937, CTA, Fonds 200, Series 487, File 477.
48. Lieutenant-Colonel R.S. Timmis, commanding, Stanley Barracks, to C.E. Chambers, May 26, 1936, CTA, Fonds 200, Series 487, File 476; R.E. Riley to C.E. Chambers, December 23, 1936, CTA, Fonds 200, Series 487, File 476.
49. R.E. Riley to C.E. Chambers, May 29, 1937, CTA, Fonds 200, Series 487, File 476.
50. C.N.E., "Official Souvenir Catalogue & Program, C.N.E., 1939," C.N.E. Archives.
51. Lieutenant-Colonel S.A. Lee, A.A. and quartermaster general, Military District No. 2, to C.E. Chambers, December 8, 1939, CTA, DPR, RG12, A, Box 46, File 7; Extract from Report No. 18 of the

Committee on Parks and Exhibitions (Board of Control Report No. 23), Adopted in Council November 8, 1940, CTA, DPR, RG12, A, Box 46, File 7.
52. Lieutenant-Colonel E.H. Shuter, "The RCR Goes to War," and "Veterans' Tales #3: 1939," available at *www.theroyalcanadianregiment.ca/history*.
53. "Elwood Hughes to aid buying soldier needs," Toronto *Telegram*, September 26, 1939, September 26, 1939 (clipping), and "Ottawa pays cost of C.N.E. changes," Toronto *Evening Telegram*, December 5, 1939 (clipping), CTA, DPR, RG12, Series A, Box 46, File 7.
54. "Canadian National Exhibition News," Toronto, July 1940, 1, C.N.E. Archives; "Canadian National Exhibition News," Toronto, February 1941, 1, 4, C.N.E. Archives; C.N.E., "Official Souvenir Catalogue & Program, C.N.E., 1940," C.N.E. Archives.
55. "Erect mess-hall and washroom, also alter building for washroom, build addition to dining-room, alterations," Department of National Defence, October 28, 1941, CTA, Fonds 200, Series 410, File 1260.
56. Superintendent's Report re: Damage to Trees, Exhibition Park, November 4, 1939, CTA, DPR, RG12, A, Box 46, File 3; commissioner of parks to Major W.E. Andres, District Engineer Office, Military District No. 2, June 7, 1940, CTA, DPR, RG12, A, Box 46, File 4.
57. Frederick Griffin, "It's Thumbs Up Year at C.N.E.," Toronto *Star Weekly*, June 28, 1941, 3, C.N.E. Archives.
58. C.N.E., "Official Souvenir Catalogue & Program, C.N.E., 1941," C.N.E. Archives. The 1941 fair drew 2,100,000 visitors, setting a new record for C.N.E. attendance. *Canadian National Exhibition News*, Toronto, Vol. 3, No. 1 (February 1942), 1.
59. *Canadian National Exhibition News, ibid.*; William A. Dryden, manager and secretary, Royal Agricultural Winter Fair, Toronto, to C.E. Chambers, January 10, 1942, CTA, Fonds 200, Series 487, File 611; "Short History Re Lease and Occupation of Stanley Barracks, 1909–1943", 788A Exhibition Park, n.d., FYA, "Stanley Barracks — General" File; D.C. Draper, chief constable, Police Department, to C.E. Chambers, December 18, 1942, CTA, DPR, RG12, Series A, Box 47, File 11, 33/50-55.
60. Major-General C.F. Constantine, deputy officer commanding,

Military District No.2, to commissioner of parks, June 11, 1943, CTA, DPR, RG12, A, Box 47, File 11, 33/50-55.
61. "Enlarge 2 windows in north wall of Manufacturer's Building", DND, January 5, 1943, CTA, Fonds 200, Series 410, File 1259.
62. "'Civvy' Street 'Office,'" *Depot News*, 2 District Depot CA(A), Vol. 2, No. 3 (September 13, 1945), 13, C.N.E. Archives, Ed Anderson Collection; "Watch Out Soldier! Danger! Booby Traps!," *The Lowdown* (published by the Public Relations Branch, Military District No. 2), Vol. No. 10, Troop Train Edition (February 20, 1946), 2, C.N.E. Archives.
63. "A Message from the Commanding Officer," *Depot News, op. cit.*; "Souvenir Pistols Prove Dangerous," *The Lowdown, op. cit.*, 3–4.
64. George Kidd, "The C.N.E. and the 2nd World War," in *Once Upon a Century, op. cit.*, 101; C.N.E., "Official Souvenir Catalogue & Program, C.N.E., 1947," C.N.E. Archives.

CHAPTER FOUR: THE POST-WAR YEARS (1945 TO TODAY)

1. J.P. Kent to C.E. Chambers, November 26 and December 30, 1946, CTA, DPR, RG12, A, Box 58, File 13.
2. "C.N.E. Stadium for 50,000 Community Centre Proposal," Toronto *Globe and Mail*, April 17, 1946, 1.
3. Bureau of Municipal Research, "The Story of Toronto's EHP," CTA, Fonds 200, Series 1365, Subseries 1, File 516; "Open Letter Issued by the Bureau of Municipal Research," Toronto, January 3, 1955, CTA, Fonds 200, Series 1365, Subseries 1, File 516.
4. Little Norway would continue to be used for emergency postwar housing until 1958. Mike Filey, *A Toronto Album 2: More Glimpses of the City That Was* (Toronto: Dundurn, 2002), 39.
5. Toronto commissioner of finance to Mayor Robert H. Saunders, June 3, 1947, CTA, Fonds 200, Series 1365, Subseries 4, File 123; Memo re: "Emergent Housing, Stanley Barracks," from G.D. Bland, July 9, 1946, CTA, Fonds 200, Series 1365, Subseries 4, File 123.
6. G.D. Bland to G.A. Lascelles, July 12, 1946, CTA, Fonds 200, Series

1365, Subseries 4, File 123; G.D. Beard, commissioner of property, to G.A. Lascelles, commissioner of finance, May 23, 1947, CTA, Fonds 200, Series 1365, Subseries 4, File 123.
7. Memo from commissioner of parks to Mayor Saunders, February 1, 1947, CTA, Fonds 200, Series 487, File 931; Board of Control, Report No. 14, Adopted in Council on April 28, 1947, CTA, Fonds 200, Series 361, Subseries 1, File 517.
8. EHP residents to City of Toronto, June 5, 1947, CTA, Fonds 200, Series 361, Subseries 1, File 517; Extract from Report No. 11 of the Committee on Property (Board of Control Report No. 19), Adopted in Council on June 10, 1947, CTA, Fonds 200, Series 487, File 931.
9. List of request to Board of Control from a group of Stanley Barracks-EHP residents, August 11, 1947, CTA, Fonds 200, Series 361, Subseries 1, File 517; Memo from A.E. Pointon, superintendent of sanitation, to Dr. G.P. Jackson, medical officer of health, May 23, 1950, CTA, Fonds 200, Series 361, Subseries 1, File 517; complaints re: heating at Stanley Barracks-EHP, CTA, Fonds 200, Series 361, Subseries 1, File 517.
10. Bland to Lascelles, April 21, 1949, CTA, Fonds 200, Series 1365, Subseries 4, File 124; Memo, Department of Public Welfare, Housing Division, re: Stanley Barracks Project, Exhibition Park, January 29, 1948, CTA, Fonds 200, Series 361, Subseries 1, File 517.
11. Handwritten note from S.E. Barnes, night watchman, Stanley Barracks, May 18, 1949, CTA, Fonds 200, Series 1365, Subseries 3, Folio 7; D. Marshall to Mr. P. Shearer, May 19, 1949, in "Stanley Barracks: Night Watchman's report, May 1949", CTA, Fonds 200, Series 1365, Subseries 3, Folio 7; "Stanley Barracks, Night Watchman's Report, September–October 1949," CTA, Fonds 200, Series 1365, Subseries 3, File 38; "Stanley Barracks, Night Watchman's report, May 1949," CTA, Fonds 200, Series 1365, Subseries 3, Folio 7.
12. "Stanley Barracks, Night Watchman's Report, September–October 1949," *op. cit.*
13. A resident of "A Annex," Stanley Barracks, to Mayor Hiram McCallum, October 2, 1949, CTA, Fonds 200, Series 361, Subseries 1, File 517; "Stanley Barracks, Night Watchman's Report, September–October 1949," *op. cit.*

14. "Stanley Barracks, Night Watchman's Report, January–February 1950," CTA, Fonds 200, Series 1365, Subseries 3, File 39; "Stanley Barracks, Night Watchman's Report, March–April 1950," CTA, Fonds 200, Series 1365, Subseries 3, File 41; "Stanley Barracks, Night Watchman's Report, November–December 1949," CTA, Fonds 200, Series 1365, Subseries 3, File 40.
15. "Stanley Barracks, Night Watchman's Report, May–June 1950," CTA, Fonds 200, Series 1365, Subseries 3, File 32.
16. H.V. Locke to D.G. Bland, May 4, 1951, CTA, Fonds 200, Series 361, Subseries 1, File 517. A few years later, Locke would come under substantial criticism from groups such as the Association of Women Electors, the Bureau of Municipal Research, and the Housing Authority, who argued that Locke's job should be taken away and his duties turned over to the Housing Authority, which would be able to move tenants out of the "sub-standard emergency housing" more quickly. Locke, who was paid partly on the basis of rent collected, depended on tenants remaining in the EHP apartments for his income. Critics argued that the city had approached the matter in the wrong way all along, and regarded EH as a financial matter, when in fact it was a welfare matter. See "Housing Head Should be Fired, Brief Charges," Toronto *Globe and Mail*, May 2, 1956, 4; correspondence, July 1956, re: rehousing of tenants currently in the EHP, and proposal re: Metro Toronto Housing Authority assumption of responsibility for all EHP and Wartime Housing, CTA, Fonds 200, Series 1365, Subseries 1, File 515.
17. "Barracks to be Razed, Families Must Move," Toronto *Globe and Mail*, January 25, 1950, 3; a Toronto woman to Mayor McCallum, November 14, 1950, CTA, Fonds 200, Series 361, Subseries 1, File 517; McCallum's response, March 12, 1951, CTA, Fonds 200, Series 361, Subseries 1, File 517.
18. "Stanley Barracks Lights OUT," Toronto *Globe and Mail*, November 14, 1950, 5.
19. Extract from Report No. 6 of the Board of Control, Adopted in Council March 5, 1951, CTA, Fonds 200, Series 487, File 931; "Demolition account, Stanley Barracks 1950-51," CTA, Fonds 200, Series 1365, Subseries 4, File 116.

STANLEY BARRACKS

20. George Weale, city clerk to Mr. G.D. Bland, commissioner of property, June 21, 1951, CTA, DPR, RG12, A, Box 81, File 3; Extract From Report No. 18 of the Board of Control Adopted in Council June 26, 1951, CTA, Fonds 200, Series 487, File 931.
21. "Last Family Moved Out, K Block to Be Wrecked At Stanley Barracks," Toronto *Globe and Mail*, August 24, 1951, 5.
22. Frederick Slade, secretary, His Majesty's Army and Navy Veterans' Society, to Robert H. Saunders, mayor, May 16, 1946, CTA, Fonds 200, Series 487, File 615.
23. Quoted by J.C. Boylen, "Significance of Stanley Barracks," Toronto *Globe and Mail*, March 1, 1953, 2, CTA, Fonds 70, Series 340, Subseries 2, File 5, "Notes on Stanley Barracks and the Denisons."
24. Ruth Hammond, "Your Gateway to Finer Living" (press release), 1957, and "The Original Gates of Historic Stanley Barracks" (press release), 1957, FYA, "Stanley Barracks — General" File.
25. J.C. Boylen, *op. cit.*; "Stanley Barracks: Home of the Musical Ride" in Toronto *Globe and Mail*, April 7, 1953, CTA, Fonds 70, Series 340, Subseries 2, File 5, "Notes on Stanley Barracks and the Denisons"; Lieutenant-Colonel W.W.G. Darling, president, R.C.M.I., to Mayor Nathan Phillips, October 25, 1956, CTA, Fonds 200, Series 361, Subseries 1, File 517.
26. Dr. Norman Found to the mayor, March 13, 1957, CTA, Fonds 200, Series 361, Subseries 1, File 517; J.M.S. Careless, letter to the editor of an unidentified newspaper, February 6, 1957, CTA, Fonds 200, Series 361, Subseries 1, File 517.
27. Brasier, *op. cit.*
28. J.A. McGinnis to chairman and Members of Toronto Civic Historical Committee, September 18, 1959, FYA, "Stanley Barracks — Restoration" File.
29. Email, Eva MacDonald, senior archaeologist/manager of historical archaeology, Archaeological Services Inc., Toronto, to author, July 30, 2010.
30. Douglas Featherling, "The Origins of Urban Canada," *Rotunda*, Vol. 22, No. 4 (Spring 1990): 51.

BIBLIOGRAPHY

Primary Sources

Archives of Ontario

Glegg, Thomas. *Notebook and Sketchbook of Thomas Glegg, 1841–1842.*

Canadian National Exhibition (C.N.E.) Archives

Canadian National Exhibition News, Toronto, July 1940, February 1941, February 1942.
Depot News, 2 District Depot CA(A), Vol. 2, No. 3 (September 13, 1945), Ed Anderson Collection.
The Lowdown, (published by the Public Relations Branch, M.D. No. 2), Vol. No. 10, Troop Train Edition (February 20, 1946).
"Official Souvenir Catalogue & Program, C.N.E." 1939, 1940, 1941, 1947.

City of Toronto Archives (CTA)

Barnes, S.E. Handwritten note from S.E. Barnes, Night Watchman, Stanley Barracks, May 18, 1949, Fonds 200, Series 1365, Subseries 3, Folio 7.

Bland, G.D., commissioner of property, to G.A. Lascelles, commissioner of finance, July 12, 1946, May 23, 1947, April 21, 1949, Fonds 200, Series 1365, Subseries 4, File 124.

Bland, G.D. Memo re: "Emergent Housing, Stanley Barracks," July 9, 1946, Fonds 200, Series 1365, Subseries 4, File 123.

Board of Control. Extract from Report No. 18 of the Committee on Parks and Exhibitions (Board of Control Report No. 23), Adopted in Council November 8, 1940, DPR, RG12, A, Box 46, File 7.

Board of Control, Report No. 14, Adopted in Council on April 28, 1947, Fonds 200, Series 361, Subseries 1, File 517.

Board of Control. Extract from Report No. 11 of the Committee on Property (Board of Control Report No. 19), Adopted in Council on June 10, 1947, Fonds 200, Series 487, File 931.

Board of Control. Extract From Report No. 18 of the Board of Control Adopted in Council June 26, 1951, Fonds 200, Series 487, File 931.

Board of Control. Extract from Report No. 6 of the Board of Control, Adopted in Council March 5, 1951, Fonds 200, Series 487, File 931.

Bradshaw, T. to Commissioner of Finance and City Treasurer, to C.E. Chambers, May 13, 1919, Fonds 200, Series 487, File 217.

Bradshaw, T. Memo to Mr. Bradshaw, Re: Garrison Common and Old Fort Property, September 24, 1918, Fonds 200, Series 487, File 217.

Bureau of Municipal Research. "The Story of Toronto's EHP." Fonds 200, Series 1365, Subseries 1, File 516.

Caldwell, E.L. (Lieutenant-Colonel), Commanding, Stanley Barracks, to C.E. Chambers, April 27, 1937, Fonds 200, Series 487, File 477.

Careless, J.M.S. Letter to the editor of an unidentified newspaper. February 6, 1957, Fonds 200, Series 361, Subseries 1, File 517.

Chambers, C.E., "Occupation of Stanley Barracks by Militia," (report). February 22, 1927, Fonds 200, Series 487, File 217.

Chetwynd, G.R. (Major) to C.E. Chambers, June 9, 1938, DPR, RG12, Series A, Box 45, File 2.

Chetwynd, G.R. (Major), RCE, to C.E. Chambers, February 10, 1936, Fonds 200, Series 487, File 476.

Chief Constable. *Journal of the Chief Constable, 1851–1852*. Municipal Records, Section A, York County, Toronto

Bibliography

City Council Minutes, Toronto, May 20, 1850, CTA (#303).

Commissioner of Finance to Mayor Robert H. Saunders, June 3, 1947, Fonds 200, Series 1365, Subseries 4, File 123.

Commissioner of Parks to Major W.E. Andres, District Engineer Office, M.D. No. 2, June 7, 1940, DPR, RG12, A, Box 46, File 4.

Commissioner of Parks to Mayor and Board of Control, July 9, 1920, Fonds 200, Series 487, File 217.

Commissioner of Parks. Memo to Mayor Saunders, February 1, 1947, Fonds 200, Series 487, File 931.

Constantine, C.R. (Major General), DOC, M.D. No.2, to Commissioner of Parks, June 11, 1943, DPR, RG12, A, Box 47, File 11, 33/50-55.

Darling, W.W.G. (Lieutenant-Colonel), President, R.C.M.I., to Mayor Nathan Phillips, October 25, 1956, Fonds 200, Series 361, Subseries 1, File 517.

"Demolition account, Stanley Barracks 1950–51," Fonds 200, Series 1365, Subseries 4, File 116.

Department of National Defence. "Enlarge 2 windows in north wall of Manufacturer's Building." January 5, 1943, Fonds 200, Series 410, File 1259.

Department of National Defence. "Erect mess-hall and washroom, also alter building for washroom, build addition to dining-room, alterations." October 28, 1941, Fonds 200, Series 410, File 1260.

Department of Parks and Recreation (DPR). Memo from DPR to Chambers. April 13, 1926, Fonds 200, Series 487, File 217.

Department of Public Welfare, Housing Division. Memo re: Stanley Barracks Project, Exhibition Park, January 29, 1948, Fonds 200, Series 361, Subseries 1, File 517.

Draper, D.C., Chief Constable, Police Department, to C.E. Chambers, December 18, 1942, DPR, RG12, Series A, Box 47, File 11, 33/50-55.

Dryden, William A. Manager and Secretary, Royal Agricultural Winter Fair, Toronto, to C.E. Chambers, January 10, 1942, Fonds 200, Series 487, File 611.

EHP residents to City of Toronto, June 5, 1947, Fonds 200, Series 361, Subseries 1, File 517.

EHP. A Toronto woman to Mayor McCallum, November 14, 1950, and

McCallum's response, Fonds 200, Series 361, Subseries 1, File 517.

EHP. Complaints re: heating at Stanley Barracks-EHP, Fonds 200, Series 361, Subseries 1, File 517.

EHP. Correspondence, July 1956, re: rehousing of tenants currently in the EHP, and proposal re: Metro Toronto Housing Authority assumption of responsibility for all EHP and Wartime Housing, Fonds 200, Series 1365, Subseries 1, File 515.

EHP. List of requests to Board of Control from a group of Stanley Barracks-EHP residents, August 11, 1947, Fonds 200, Series 361, Subseries 1, File 517.

EHP. Resident of "A Annex," Stanley Barracks, to Mayor Hiram McCallum, October 2, 1949, Fonds 200, Series 361, Subseries 1, File 517.

Found, Dr. Norman, to the Mayor, March 13, 1957, Fonds 200, Series 361, Subseries 1, File 517.

Gilman, Lieutenant-Colonel to Mr. C.E. Chambers, Commissioner of Parks, March 22, 1922, Fonds 200, Series 487, File 217.

Gilman, Lieutenant-Colonel to Mr. C.E. Chambers, Commissioner of Parks, March 27, 1922, DPR, RG12, A, Box 19, File 5.

Grant-Suttie, G.L.P. (Captain) to C.E. Chambers, April 10, 1922, Fonds 200, Series 487, File 217.

High Bailiff. Journal of the High Bailiff 1849–1851, Municipal Records, Section A, York County, Toronto.

Kent, J.P. to C.E. Chambers, November 26 and December 30, 1946, DPR, RG12, A, Box 58, File 13.

Lee, S.A. (Lieutenant-Colonel), Acting Adjutant and Quartermaster General, Military District No. 2, to C.E. Chambers, December 8, 1939, DPR, RG12, A, Box 46, File 7.

Littlejohn, W.A., City Clerk, to C.E. Chambers, May 28, 1920, January 12, 1927, February 18, 1927, Fonds 200, Series 487, File 217.

Locke, H.V. to D.G. Bland, May 4, 1951, Fonds 200, Series 361, Subseries 1, File 517.

Love. Memo, Mr. Love to Mr. Chambers, May 29, 1940, DPR, RG12, A, Box 45, File 3.

Marshall, D. to Mr. P. Shearer, May 19, 1949, in "Stanley Barracks: Night

Bibliography

Watchman's report, May 1949," Fonds 200, Series 1365, Subseries 3, Folio 7.

"Open Letter Issued by the Bureau of Municipal Research," Toronto, January 3, 1955, Fonds 200, Series 1365, Subseries 1, File 516.

Pointon, A.E., Superintendent of Sanitation. Memo to Dr. G.P. Jackson, Medical Officer of Health, May 23, 1950, Fonds 200, Series 361, Subseries 1, File 517.

Riley, R.E. to C.E. Chambers, December 23, 1936, May 29, 1937, Fonds 200, Series 487, File 476.

Slade, Frederick, Secretary, His Majesty's Army and Navy Veterans' Society, to Robert H. Saunders, Mayor, May 16, 1946, Fonds 200, Series 487, File 615.

"Stanley Barracks, Night Watchman's Report, May 1949," Fonds 200, Series 1365, Subseries 3, Folio 7.

"Stanley Barracks, Night Watchman's Report, September–October 1949," Fonds 200, Series 1365, Subseries 3, File 38.

"Stanley Barracks, Night Watchman's Report, November–December 1949," Fonds 200, Series 1365, Subseries 3, File 40.

"Stanley Barracks, Night Watchman's Report, January–February 1950," Fonds 200, Series 1365, Subseries 3, File 39.

"Stanley Barracks, Night Watchman's Report, March–April 1950," Fonds 200, Series 1365, Subseries 3, File 41.

"Stanley Barracks, Night Watchman's Report, May–June 1950," Fonds 200, Series 1365, Subseries 3, File 32.

Superintendent's Report re Damage to Trees, Exhibition Park, November 4, 1939, DPR, RG12, A, Box 46, File 3.

Timmis, R.S. (Lieutenant-Colonel), Commanding, Stanley Barracks, to C.E. Chambers, May 26, 1936, Fonds 200, Series 487, File 476.

Waters, H.W. Assistant Manager and Secretary, C.N.E. Association, to C.E. Chambers, Commissioner of Parks, January 19, 1927, DPR, RG12, A, Box 21, File 6.

Waters, H.W. to C.E. Chambers, January 19, 1927, Fonds 200, Series 487, File 217.

Weale, George, City Clerk to Mr. G.D. Bland, Commissioner of Property, June 21, 1951, DPR, RG12, A, Box 81, File 3.

Fort York Archives (FYA)

"Agreement re: Stanley Barracks & Eastern Entrance to Canadian National Exhibition, 27th June 1927, Between His Majesty the King represented by The Hon. The Minister of National Defence of Canada and The Corporation of the City of Toronto," "Stanley Barracks — General" File.

"Inscriptions of tablets outside main grouping," Strachan Avenue Cemetery.

"Short History Re: Lease and Occupation of Stanley Barracks, 1909–1943", 788A Exhibition Park, n.d., "Stanley Barracks — General" File.

Brasier, Dorothy Caroline Steer. "Stanley Barracks, Toronto, Ont. — Memories." Unpublished account, May 25, 1985, "Stanley Barracks — General" File.

J.A. McGinnis to Chairman and Members of Toronto Civic Historical Committee, September 18, 1959, "Stanley Barracks — Restoration" File.

Glenbow Museum Archives (GMA)

Bagley, Fred A. *The '74 Mounties*. Unpublished manuscript, 1938. Fred A. Bagley Papers, M43, Ch. II, p. 6.

Parker, William. *Thirty Eight and a Half Years Service and Experience in the Mounties*. Unpublished manuscript, n.d., William Parker Papers, M934, File 22, Ch. II.

Parker, William. Diary of William Parker 1874. William Parker Papers, M934, File 1.

Parker, William. William Parker Papers, M934, Files 6, 22.

Library and Archives of Canada (LAC):

Adjutant General, Canadian Militia, circular letter to GOC, 2nd Division, November 21, 1914, RG24, Vol. 4287, 34-1-26, Vol. 1.

Bibliography

Anonymous to the Prime Minister, April 2, 1918, RG24, Vol. 2023, File HQC-965, 193–97.

"Annual Report of the Detachment 1st Battalion 60th Royal Rifles stationed at Toronto," McGrigor Papers, MG 40, F1 Vol. 2.

"A Soldier" to Brigadier-General Gunn, General Officer Commanding, Military District No. 2, February 9, 1919, RG24, Vol. 4353, 34-5-44, Vol. 2.

Baldwin, L.H. to W.D. Otter, June 25, 1888, RG9, IIA1, Vol. 211, File A7712.

Bimburg, Paul to Lieutenant-Colonel Elliott, February 6, 1915, Vol. 4276, 34-1-3, Vol. 5.

Boulton, William H. Sir Richard Jackson, Commander of the Forces, January 24, 1845, RG8, "C" Series, Vol. 519, 216–18.

Byham, R., Office of Ordnance, to Inspector General of Fortifications, June 14, 1839, W.O. 55, Vol. 874.

Coffin, William F. Commissioner of Ordnance and Admiralty Lands, to E.A. Meredith, Deputy of the Minister of the Interior, July 13, 1874, RG9, IIA1, Vol. 64, File 9994.

Coffin, William F. to E.A. Meredith, Department of the Minister of the Interior, July 13, 1874, and Lieutenant-Colonel W. Powell, Acting Adjutant General of Militia, to Minister of Militia and Defence, August 7, 1874, RG9, IIA1, Vol. 64, File 9994.

Commanding Officer, No. 2 R.D., Royal Canadian Regiment, Stanley Barracks, Toronto, to Deputy Officer Commanding, Military District No. 2, February 16, 1900, RG9, IIA1, Vol. 327, File 18729.

Cornwall, H., Barrack Master, to the Respective Officers, May 18, 1842, RG8, "C" Series, Vol. 595, 138.

Crush, George A. (Sergeant) March 24, 1874 to Lieutenant-Colonel Goodwin, Military Storekeeper, Toronto, RG9, IIA1, Vol. 59, File 9226.

Desbarats, G.J., Acting Deputy Minister, Department of National Defence, to the Deputy Minister, Department of Justice, Ottawa, May 15, 1923, RG13, Vol. 278, File 1923-940.

Durie, William. Telegram to Colonel Powell, September 8, 1879, RG9, IIA1, Vol. 99, File 05922.

Durie, William. Report from Lieutenant-Colonel Durie, Deputy Adjutant

General, Military District No. 2, Old Fort, Toronto, to the Acting Adjutant General of Militia, Headquarters, Ottawa, March 4, 1874, RG9, IIA1, Vol. 59, File 9226.

Edwards, W., Secretary, Electoral Division Society, to Sir George E. Cartier, Minister of Militia, September 1, 1869, RG9, IIA1, Vol. 12, File 1849.

Elliot, Lieutenant-Colonel to Captain R.S. Wilson, 48th Highlanders, February 9, 1915, Vol. 4276, 34-1-3, Vol. 5.

Fraser, A. Mackenzie. Report by A. Mackenzie Fraser, Deputy Quartermaster General's Office, Montreal, June 26, 1847, RG8, "C" Series, Vol. 31, 85–86.

Freeling, A.H. Diary of Lieutenant Arthur Henry Freeling, R.E., 67/141.

General Officer Commanding, 2nd Division. Memo to Secretary, Military Council, August 24, 1914, and September 8, 1914, RG24, Vol. 4276, 34-1-3, Vol. 1.

General Officer Commanding, Correspondence, re: "That the sanitary condition of the New Fort Barracks and of the buildings at the Old Fort, Toronto, is most unsatisfactory, August 30, October 6, December 19, December 26, and December 28, 1892, RG9, IIA1, Vol. 263, File A12272.

Goodwin, Lieutenant-Colonel to Lieutenant-Colonel Thomas Wily, February 16, 1874, RG9, IIA1, Vol. 59, File 9226.

Goodwin, Lieutenant-Colonel to Lieutenant-Colonel Wily, March 24, 1874, RG9, IIA1, Vol. 59, File 9226.

Gzowski, C.S. to Robert B. Denison, August 10, 1872, and Robert B. Denison, Acting Deputy Adjutant General to the Deputy Adjutant General of Militia, Ottawa, August 13, 1872, RG9, IIA1, Vol. 43, File 6952.

Gzowski, C.S. to Sir George E. Cartier, Minister of Militia and Defence, Ottawa, August 27, 1870, RG9, IIA1, Vol. 23, File 3786.

Hamilton, James to Adolphe Caron, March 12, 1888, RG9, IIA1, Vol. 211, File A7712.

Hemtzman, F.C. Inspection Report by Lieutenant F.C. Hemtzman, Camp Field Officer of the Day, RG24, Vol. 4354, 34-5-44, Vol. 1.

Irwin, D. (Major) to Lieutenant-Colonel Powell, Acting Adjutant General, Ottawa, February 10, 1874, RG9, IIA1, Vol. 59, File 9203.

Bibliography

Lee, Percival J., Area Supervisor, Y.M.C.A., to Major General W.A. Logie, Officer Commanding, Military District No. 2, November 16, 1917, RG24, Vol. 4349, 34-5-12.

Lessard, F.L. to Deputy Officer Commanding, Military District No. 2, October 18, 1899, RG9, IIA1, Vol. 319, File 17888.

Major T. Foster *et al.* to Military Secretary, Headquarters, May 30, 1842, RG8, C Series, Vol. 595, 141.

McLean, J.B. (Captain), Royal Grenadiers, to Lieutenant-Colonel George B. Dawson, Commanding Royal Grenadiers, June 27, 1888, RG9, IIA1, Vol. 211, File A7712.

Memo from Lieutenant-Colonel Thomas Wily, Director of Stores, August 1, 1871, RG9, IIA1, Vol. 32, File 3204.

Memo to Officer in care of Troops, Exhibition Camp, January 29, 1919, RG24, Vol. 4354, 43-5-4, Vol. 1.

Memo, April 5, 1918, RG24, Vol. 4353, 34-5-44, Vol. 1.

Memo, Department of Militia and Defence, June 25, 1870, RG9, IIA1, Vol. 21, File 3399.

Memo, May 3, 1918, RG24, Vol. 4353, 34-5-44, Vol. 1.

Memo, September 7, 1914, RG24, Vol. 4276, 34-1-3, Vol. 1.

Murdoch (Chief Secretary) to Lieutenant-Colonel O'Donnell, Military Secretary, March 3, 1840, RG8, C Series, Vol. 592, 85–86.

Newcombe, E.L. to Acting Deputy Minister, Department of National Defence, Ottawa, September 12, 1923, RG13, Vol. 278, File 1923-940.

Nicolls, Gustavus. "Estimate of the probable expense of Constructing a Barrack Establishment at Toronto, revised for 300 Men, from the Plans & Estimates forwarded by Colonel Nicolls on the December 28, 1833 amounting to £22,853.6.7 ¼ ," London, February 28, 1839, W.O. 55, Vol. 874.

Ontario Rifle Association Lease, 1881, RG9, IIA1, Vol. 124, File 08902.

Order in Council (Privy Council), March 1, 1899, RG9, IIA1, Vol. 314, File 17420 ½.

Otter, W.D. "Illuminated Address from the City of Toronto, March 1885," MG30, E242.

Otter, W.D. (Lieutenant-Colonel) to the Minister of Militia and Defence, March 13, 1878, RG9, IIA1, Vol. 88, File 04291.

Otter, W.D. to Powell, June 30, 1888, RG9, IIA1, Vol. 211, File A7712.

Otter, W.D. to Lieutenant-Colonel Panet, Deputy of the Minister of Militia, December 16, 1881, RG9, IIA1, Vol. 118, File 08188.

Proceeding of Board of Inquiry into death of #537 Yousseff Hussein, held at Stanley Barracks, April 1, 1916, RG24, Vol. 4279, 34-1-3, Vol. 11.

"Proceedings of a Court of Inquiry Assembled at New Fort Barracks, Toronto on the 13th September 1887," RG9, IIA1, Vol. 205, File A7124.

"Report and Estimate of the Probable Expense of Constructing Ball Courts at the Principal Military Stations in Canada," Royal Engineers Office, Montreal, January 13, 1842, W.O. 55, Vol. 877.

"Report and Estimate of the probable expense of Various Services proposed to Complete The New Barrack Establishment at Toronto Canada," December 29, 1841, W.O. 55, Vol. 877, 357–69.

"Report on the Canada Barracks visited and inspected in Oct. 1863 by Lt.-Col. Jervois and Capt. R. Harrison," RG8, Series II, Vol. 34, 47, 102–07.

Report re: Prisoners at Stanley Barracks, October 15, 1914, RG24, Vol. 4276, 34-1-3, Vol. 2. GOC, 2nd Division to Otter, December 17, 1914, RG24, Vol. 4276, 34-1-3, Vol.4.

Report re: Stanley Barracks Internment Station, OC, M.D. No. 2, to Otter, December 16, 1914, RG24, Vol. 4287, 34-1-26, Vol. 1.

"Report — Toronto — New Barrack Establishment," June 9, 1841, W.O. 55, Vol. 876.

Robertson-Ross, P. to Minister of Militia and Defence, September 3, 1870, RG9, IIA1, Vol. 23, File 3786.

"Schedule of POW handed over to the Department of Militia by the RNWM Police for Internment," May 1917, RG18, Vol. 519, File RCMP 1917, No. 10, Part I.

Scoble, Thomas A. to Lieutenant-Colonel Wily, Director of Stores, April 28, 1874, RG9, IIA1, Vol. 59, File 9226.

Scoble, Thomas A., telegram to Lieutenant-Colonel Wily, February 16, 1874; Scoble to Wily, Director of Stores, Ottawa, March 13, 1874; Memo from Wily, March 16, 1874; and Memo from Wily, April 17, 1874, RG9, IIA1, Vol. 59, File 9226.

Selby-Smyth, E. (Major-General) to Minister of Militia and Defence, March 10, 1875, RG9, IIA1, Vol. 71, File 01270.

Selby-Smyth, E. (Major-General) to the Minister of Militia and Defence, March 10, 1875, RG9, IIA1, Vol. 71, File 01270.

Selby-Smyth, E. Memo from Major-General E. Selby-Smyth, April 13, 1880, RG9, IIA1, Vol. 103, File 06415.

Shaw, John, Mayor of Toronto, to Dr. Borden, Minister of Militia, September 23, 1897, RG9, IIA1, Vol. 302, File 16187.

Slatter, John, President, Toronto Orchestral Association, to Adolphe Caron, Minister of Militia and Defence, October 2, 1891, RG9, IIA1, Vol. 254, File A11436.

Spark, R. (Lieutenant-Colonel) to H. Cornwall, Barrack Office, Toronto, May 17, 1842, RG8, "C" Series, Vol. 595, 139.

Story, R.W. (Captain) R.A., Vincent Biscoe, R.E., and J.A. Harvey, Department of Ordnance, to the Respective Officer of Ordnance, Toronto, May 23, 1842, RG8, "C" Series, Vol. 595, 137.

Wily, Thomas (Lieutenant-Colonel) to the Minister of Militia and Defence, September 30, 1870, RG9, IIA1, File 3432.

Wily, Thomas. Report from Lieutenant-Colonel Thomas Wily to the Minister of Militia and Defence, July 21, 1870, RG9, IIA1, Vol. 21, File 3432.

Metropolitan Toronto Reference Library (MTPL), Baldwin Room

Laurier, Wilfrid to J.O. Thorn, March 30, 1909, Old Fort Protective Association (OFPA) Papers.

"Memoranda upon the nature and value of Materials, as also on Labour in Canada from information in the Office of the Commanding R. Engineer," 1841.

Otter, W.D. (General) to Major J.W. Thomas, Secretary, OFPA, March 7, 1908, OFPA Papers.

Timmis, R.S. Timmis Diaries. Reginald Symonds Timmis Fonds, S249.

National Library of Scotland

Elliot, Gilbert. Journal of Gilbert Elliot, MS. 11764, MS. 12016.
Elliot, Gilbert. Letters of Gilbert Elliot, MS. 11901, MS. 11782, MS. 11783, MS. 11764.

Prince Edward County Archives

Baines, Harry E. "A Month's Leave, or, The Cruise of the *Breeze*" (Diary of Harry E. Baines).

Thomas Fisher Rare Book Library, University of Toronto

Mackenzie, William Orde. Dr. William Orde Mackenzie's Canadian Diary, Mss. 5274.

United States Military Academy, Special Collections Archives

Knowlton, Minor (Lieutenant)."Copy of a Report on the Military Establishments of the British Provinces," December 3, 1840. Transcription by Carl Benn. Published in *The York Pioneer*, Vol. 98, 2003.

Secondary Sources

Alexander, James E. *Passages in the Life of a Soldier; or, Military Service in the East and West*. Vol. I. London: Hurst and Blackett, 1857.
Atkin, Ronald. *Maintain the Right: The Early History of the North West Mounted Police, 1873–1900*. Toronto: Macmillan, 1973.
Bailey, W.J. and E.R. Toop. *Canadian Military Post Offices to 1986*. Toronto: Unitrade Press, 1987.

Bibliography

Benn, Carl. "Toronto's Forgotten Fort." Unpublished article. Fort York Archives, File "Stanley Barracks — General."

___. *Historic Fort York 1793–1993.* Toronto: Natural Heritage/Natural History Inc., 1993.

Boudreau, Joseph A. "The Enemy Alien Problem in Canada, 1914–1921." Ph.D. diss. UCLA, 1965.

Camp, A.D. and L.F. Atkins. *7th Toronto Regiment, Royal Regiment of Canadian Artillery 1866–1966.* Toronto: 7th Toronto Regiment, RCA, n.d.

"The Canadian Military International Horse Show Team, 1927, By 'Eye Witness.'" *Canadian Defence Quarterly,* Vol. V (October 1927–July 1928).

Chambers, Ernest J. *The Royal North-West Mounted Police: A Corps History.* Montreal and Ottawa: Mortimer Press, 1906.

Coats, Robert H. "The Alien Enemy in Canada: Internment Operations." In *Canada in the Great War* by Various Authorities. Vol. II. Toronto: United Publishers of Canada Limited, 1919.

Craick, William A. "Notes from Toronto Newspapers." Vol. 27.

Craufurd-Lewis, Michael. *Macleod of the Mounties: The North American Saga as seen through the life of a Scottish Canadian Hero.* Ottawa: The Golden Dog Press, 1999.

D'Artigue, Jean. *Six Years in the Canadian North-West.* Toronto: Hunter, Rose and Company, 1882.

"The Defence of Canada." *Blackwood's Edinburgh Magazine,* Vol. XCI, No. DLVI, February 1862, 228–58.

Dempsey, Hugh A. *William Parker: Mounted Policeman.* Edmonton: Hurtig, 1973.

Denison, George T. *Soldiering in Canada: Recollections and Experiences.* 2nd edition. Toronto: George N. Morang and Company Limited, 1901.

Denny, Cecil E. *The Law Marches West.* Edited by W.B. Cameron. Toronto: J.M. Dent and Sons, 1972.

___. *The Riders of the Plains: A Reminiscence of the Early and Exciting Days in the North West.* Calgary: The Herald Company, Limited, 1905.

Duncan, Francis. *Our Garrisons in the West or Sketches in British North America.* London: Chapman and Hall, 1864.

Featherling, Douglas. "The Origins of Urban Canada." *Rotunda*, Vol.22, No. 4 (Spring 1990).

Fetherstonhaugh, R.C. *The Royal Canadian Regiment 1883–1933*. Canada: The Royal Canadian Regiment, 1936.

Filey, Mike. *A Toronto Album 2: More Glimpses of the City That Was.* Toronto: Dundurn, 2002.

Firth, Edith, ed. *The Town of York 1793–1815: A Collection of Documents of Early Toronto.* Toronto: Champlain Society/University of Toronto, 1962.

___, ed. *The Town of York 1815–1834: A Further Collection of Documents of Early Toronto.* Toronto: Champlain Society/University of Toronto Press, 1966.

Goldring, Philip. "The First Contingent: The North-West Mounted Police, 1873–74." In *Canadian Historic Sites: Occasional Papers in Archaeology and History No. 21*. Ottawa: Parks Canada, 1979.

Greenhous, Brereton. *Dragoon*. Belleville, ON: Guild of the Royal Canadian Dragoons, 1983.

Hammond, Ruth. "The Original Gates of Historic Stanley Barracks." Press release, Guildwood Village, 1957.

___. "Your Gateway to Finer Living." Press release, Guildwood Village, 1957.

Harris, Stephen J. *Canadian Brass: The Making of a Professional Army, 1860–1939*. Toronto: University of Toronto Press, 1988.

Harvison, C.W. *The Horsemen*. Toronto and Montreal: McClelland & Stewart, 1967.

Haydon, A.L. *The Riders of the Plains: A Record of the Royal North-West Mounted Police of Canada, 1873–1910.* Edmonton: Hurtig, 1971.

Hopkins, J. Castell. *The Canadian Annual Review of Public Affairs: 1914.* Toronto: Annual Review Publishing Company, 1915.

Horall, S.W. "Sir John A. Macdonald and the Mounted Police Force for the Northwest Territories." *Canadian Historical Review* LIII (1972).

___. "The March West." *Men in Scarlet*. Edited by Hugh A. Dempsey. Calgary: Historical Society of Alberta/McClelland & Stewart West, n.d.

___. *The Pictorial History of the Royal Canadian Mounted Police*. Toronto: McGraw-Hill Ryerson Limited, 1973.

Kelly, Nora, and William Kelly. *The Royal Canadian Mounted Police: A Century of History 1873–1973*. Edmonton: Hurtig, 1973.

Kidd, George. "The C.N.E. and the 2nd World War." In *Once Upon a Century: 100 Year History of the "Ex."* Toronto: J.H. Robinson Publishing Limited, 1978.

Killan, Gerald. *Preserving Ontario's Past*. Ottawa: Love Printing Service Limited, 1976.

Luciuk, Lubomyr. *In Fear of the Barbed Wire Fence: Canada's First National Internment Operations and the Ukrainian Canadians, 1914–1920*. Kingston: Kashtan Press, 2001.

MacBeth, R.G. *Policing the Plains, Being the Real-Life Record of the Famous North-West Mounted Police*. London: Hodder and Staughton, 1922.

Macleod, R.C. *The N.W.M.P. and Law Enforcement 1873–1905*. Toronto: University of Toronto Press, 1976.

Middleton, J.E. "Canadian War Camps." In *Canada in the Great War* by Various Authorities. Vol. II. Toronto: United Publishers of Canada Limited, 1919.

Morton, Desmond. "Sir William Otter and Internment Operations in Canada during the First World War." *Canadian Historical Review*, Vol. LV, No. 1 (March 1974).

___. *The Canadian General: Sir William Otter*. Toronto: Hakkert, 1974.

Otter, William D. *The Guide: a manual for the Canadian militia (infantry), embracing the interior economy, duties, discipline, dress, books and correspondence of a regiment in barracks, camp, or at home, with bugle calls and instructions for transport, pitching tents, etc.* Toronto: Willing and Williamson, 1880.

Pedro, Dom. *Sketches*. Toronto: self-published, 1891.

Preston, Richard A. "Military Influence on the Development of Canada." In *The Canadian Military: A Profile*. Edited by Hector J. Massey, Canada: Copp Clark, 1972.

Roberts, V.M. "Memorabilia — Being a Collection of Extracts Relating to the Origin of the Name Toronto, and the History of the Water Front of the City, its Harbour and Shipping, from 1669 to 1912. Gathered from Standard Authorities and Newspapers," (Vol. V): 3, Toronto Harbour Commission Archives.

Robertson, John Ross. *Robertson's Landmarks of Toronto: A Collection of Historical Sketches of the Old Town of York from 1792 until 1833, and of Toronto from 1834 to 1893*. Vol. I. Toronto: J. Ross Robertson, 1894.

Russell, W. Howard. *Canada: Its Defences, Condition, and Resources, Being a Second and Concluding Volume of "My Diary, North and South."* 2nd edition. Boston: T.O.H.P. Burnham, 1865.

Shea, Kevin, and John Jason Wilson. *Lord Stanley: The Man Behind the Cup*. Bolton, ON: Fenn, 2006.

Shuter, E.H. "The RCR Goes to War." Available at *www.theroyalcanadianregiment.ca*.

___. "Veteran's Tales #2 — Toronto: Stanley Barracks in the 1930s." Available at *www.theroyalcanadianregiment.ca*.

___. "Veterans' Tales #3: 1939." Available at *www.theroyalcanadianregiment.ca/history*.

Spencer, Dudley D. "Bucephalus." *Pro Patria*, No. 9 (August 1971). Available at *www.theroyalcanadianregiment.ca*.

Stacey, C.P. *Canada and the British Army 1846-1871: A Study in the Practice of Responsible Government*. Revised ed. Toronto: University of Toronto Press, 1963.

Stanley, George F.G. "Military Education in Canada, 1867-1970." In *The Canadian Military: A Profile*. Edited by Hector J. Massey. Canada: Copp Clark, 1972.

___. *Canada's Soldiers 1604–1954: The Military History of an Unmilitary People*. Toronto: Macmillan, 1954.

___. *Toil and Trouble: Military Expeditions to Red River*. Canadian War Museum Publication No. 25. Toronto and Oxford: Dundurn, 1989.

Steele, Samuel B. *Forty Years in Canada: Reminiscences of the Great North-West with Some Account of His Service in South Africa*. New York: Dodd, Mead and Company, 1915.

Wallace, Jim. *A Double Duty: The Decisive First Decade of the North West Mounted Police*. Winnipeg: Bunker to Bunker Books, 1997.

Wilson, Barbara M., ed. *Ontario and the First World War 1914–1918: A Collection of Documents*. Toronto: University of Toronto Press, 1977.

Withrow, John. "Born Out of Protest." In *Once Upon a Century: 100 Year History of the "Ex."* Toronto: J.H. Robinson Publishing Limited, 1978.

Bibliography

Worthington, Clara Ellen. *"The Spur and the Sprocket": The Story of the Royal Canadian Dragoons.* CFB Gagetown, NB: Royal Canadian Dragoons, 1968.

Newspapers

Aurora *Banner*
Toronto *Daily Globe*
Toronto *Daily World*
Toronto *Evening Globe*
Toronto *Evening Telegram*
Toronto *Globe*
Toronto *Globe and Mail*
Toronto *Globe Pictorial Supplement*
Toronto *Mail*
Toronto *Star Weekly*
Toronto *Sunday World*
Toronto *Telegram*

Interviews and Personal Correspondence

Snell, Carol. Interview, February 23, 1990.
Campbell, Lois. Interviews, April 26 and 27, 1989.
Collins, Doris E. Letter to author, May 7, 1989.
Johnson, Ed. Letter to author, August 1, 1989.
Maxted, Mary. Interview, February 3, 1988.
MacDonald, Eva. Senior Archaeologist/Manager of Historical Archaeology, Archaeological Services Inc., Toronto. Email to author, July 30, 2010.

STANLEY BARRACKS

Maps and Plans

1841: "New Barrack Establishment Toronto, as completed" by Captain Vincent Biscoe, R.E., December 2, 1841, LAC, NMC-5394.

1841: "New Barrack Establishment, Toronto, as Completed," Vincent Biscoe, Captain, R.E., December 2, 1841, LAC, NMC-5394.

1850: "Toronto, C.W. — Map showing the Military Reserves containing about 182 Acres exclusive of the portion leased to the Corporation." Henry William Vavasour, Colonel Commanding R. Engineers Canada and W.F. Lambert, Lieutenant, R. Engineers, 1850. MTPL, Special Collections.

1851: "Toronto — Sketch of the Ordnance Property showing the portion tinted yellow which is recommended by Major Tullock Superintendent of Pensioners to be sold for the purpose of defraying the expense of draining the remaining portion of the Reserve," F.W. Whingates, Lieutenant-Colonel Commanding, R. Engineers, September 18, 1851, MTPL.

1852: "Canada, Toronto, Plan shewing the Boundaries as marked on the ground of the Military Reserve belonging to the Ordnance in the City of Toronto, County and Township of York, Canada West, as Surveyed by Mr. Sandford Fleming, Provincial Land Surveyor, between the months of Novr. 1851 & May 1852," LAC, 11449, (R) H1/440/Toronto/1852.

1852: "Toronto C.W." (detail), by Lieutenant A.R. Vyvyan Crease, R.E., January 1852, LAC, NMC, P/440-Toronto-1852.

1858: "Plan of the City of Toronto," drawn by Charles Unwin, P.L. Surveyor, 1858, MTPL.

1868: "Relative Sketch Shewing the Position of the Batteries," LAC, NMC, H4/440-Toronto-1868-No. 1.

1879: "Map of Toronto," P. Jamieson Clothier, Yonge and Queen Streets, 1879, MTPL.

1889: "Plan of Buildings used as Officer's Quarters, New Fort Barracks, Toronto," 1889, LAC, C-6847.

1895: "City of Toronto," published by Might Directory Co., prepared in the office of John Galt, C.E. and M.E., 1895, MTPL.

Bibliography

1895: "Toronto New Barracks &c.," Owen Staples, 1895. Copy of original plans of Stanley Barracks, New Fort, Toronto, 1840, from drawing by Walkem of Royal Engineers. MTPL, T-14118.

1898: "Plan of the City of Toronto," City Engineer's Office, 1898, MTPL.

1906: "Canadian National Exhibition Grounds and Buildings, 1906," 912.713541 1906, Ward 4 Small, MTPL.

1912: "Waterfront Development," The Toronto Harbour Commissioners Engineering Department, 1912, MTPL.

1915: "Floor Plan of Subdivided Buildings, Stanley Barracks, Toronto," by Major Lawrence Buchan, RRCI, January 19, 1894, LAC, NMC, C-49451; "Stanley Barracks, Toronto", by Lieutenant. H .J. Burden, 9th M.H., May 7, 1915, FYA, 1989.31.35.b.

1925: "Lloyd's Map of Greater Toronto and Suburbs," by the Map Company, Toronto, 1925. MTPL.

1939: "Plan Showing Accommodation at Exhibition Park," DND, M.D. No. 2, October 27, 1939. Revised by L.S. Woolnaugh, Sergeant R.C.E., December 29, 1939. Revised by Wells, December 11, 1942. C.N.E. Archives, Ed Anderson Collection.

INDEX

Adelaide Street (Toronto), 107, 108
Aitkin, Alexander, 15, 16, 18
Alexandra Studio (Toronto), 124
Aldershot, England, 91, 92
Alexander, Sir James E., 25, 161
Alger, Lieutenant-Colonel __, 73
American Civil War, 37, 44, 57
Asylum, *see* Provincial Lunatic Asylum

Bagley, Fred, 57, 61–63, 65, 168
Baines, Lieutenant Harry Egerton, 38, 39, 164
Baldwin, L.H., 81, 171
Band, regimental, 26, 28, 30, 61, 65, 78
Beatty, Russell, 148
Beatty Family, 148
Bell, Alderman Thomas, 33
Bell, Lieutenant-Colonel Walker, 121, 122
Biscoe, Captain Vincent, 21, 24, 25, 160, 161
Board of Control (City of Toronto), 128, 144, 148, 149, 173, 177, 186
Bootlegging: 118
    Reported at Stanley Barracks, 146
Borden, Sir Frederick, 90, 171, 173
Borden, Prime Minister Robert, 93, 113
Boulton, Mayor William H., 35, 163
Boundary disputes with United States:
    Maine–New Brunswick, 25
    Oregon, 25
Brasier, Dorothy Caroline (Steer), 154, 178

Breeze (yacht), 38, 39, 164
"Bucephalus" (horse), 115–17
Burden, Lieutenant H.J., 110, 176
Butler, Lieutenant W.F., 52

CEF, *see* Canadian Expeditionary Force
C.N.E., *see* Canadian National Exhibition
C.N.E. Association, *see* Canadian National Exhibition
C.N.E. Camp, 97, 98, 101, 105, 129–39
CWAC, *see* Canadian Women's Army Corps, 136
Caldwell, Lieutenant-Colonel E.L., 127, 179
Camp Borden, 141
Campbell, Lois, 173, 201
Canadian Army International Jumping Team, 115, 117
Canadian Expeditionary Force (First World War), 11
Canadian Field Artillery (15th Battery), 94
Canadian General: Sir William Otter, The, 72, 164–65
Canadian Legion, 127, 128
Canadian Mounted Rifles, 86, 87
Canadian Militia, 34, 52, 54, 66, 72, 75, 157, 175
Canadian National Exhibition (C.N.E.), 8, 11, 12, 67, 88, 89, 93–106, 116, 120–22, 124, 125, 129–31, 134, 136–39, 141, 143–45, 147, 150, 151,

154, 155, 173, 179, 180, 181
Annual fair, 129, 139
Buildings, 8, 36, 38, 67, 93, 94, 98, 129, 136, 155
Grandstand, grandstand show, 88, 94, 103, 125, 129, 132, 137–39
Grounds (Exhibition Park, Exhibition Place), 7, 8, 11, 67, 69, 79, 88, 89, 93, 94, 98, 99, 100, 101, 104, 109, 114–16, 118, 121, 122, 124, 127, 129, 135, 141, 143, 146, 151, 154–56
Rollercoaster, 98, 102, 125
Canadian National Exhibition Association, 11, 69, 90, 93, 121, 122, 130, 155, 174, 178
Canadian Regiment of Infantry, 82
Canadian Sports Hall of Fame, 155
Canadian Women's Army Corps (CWAC), 135–36
Careless, J.M.S., 153, 184
Carleton, Sir Guy (Lord Dorchester), 15
Caroline Affair, 9
Caron, Adolphe (Minister of Militia) 70, 71, 76, 78, 80, 170, 171
Carter, Doris E., *see* Doris Collins
Carter, Lois, *see* Lois Campbell
Carter, Colour Sergeant William Charles, 90, 91, 173
Carvell, Superintendent Jacob, (North-West Mounted Police), 57
Cavalry School Corps, 8, *see also* Royal Canadian Dragoons
Cemetery, military, *see also* Strachan Avenue Cemetery, 37, 89
Chambers, Commissioner C.E., 127, 128, 177–81
Chetwynd, Major G.R., 126, 127, 179
Chicago World's Fair (1893), 88
City Council (Toronto), 33, 36, 67, 88, 89, 136, 147, 155, 156
Civil War, *see* American Civil War
Clay, Gunner, __, ("A" Battery, RCA), 50
Coatsworth, Judge Emerson, 107
Coffin, William F., 66, 163, 169
Colborne, Lieutenant Governor Sir John, 17, 20, 160

Collingwood, Ontario, 43
Collins, Doris (Carter), 90, 173, 201
Confederation, 105
Cooper, James Fenimore, 56, 61, 64
Cornwall and York, Duke and Duchess of, 88
Cornwall, H. (Barrack Master), 161
Cricket, cricket ground, 23, 24, 26, 28, 61, 64, 69
Cricket Club, *see* Toronto Cricket Club
Crimean War, 36, 57
Crush, Sergeant George A., 49, 51, 166
Crystal Palace (Exhibition Grounds), 36, 38, 43, 67, 95
Cypress Hills Massacre (1873), 53–54

d'Artigue, Jean, 55, 56, 61, 63–65, 167, 169
Darling, Lieutenant-Colonel W.W.G., 152, 153, 184
Death of Turkish prisoner at Stanley Barracks internment station, 1916, *see* Hussein, Youssef
Defence Purchasing Board of Canada, 129
Demobilization, demobilization centre, 99, 105, 115, 136
Denison, George T., 34, 163
Denison, Robert B., 49, 165
Denny, Captain Cecil E., 64, 167
Dental Corps, 129
Department of the Interior, 66
Department of National Defence, 122, 124, 136, 142
Department of Militia and Defence, 38, 46–49, 51, 62, 66, 67, 89, 114, 177
Department of Munitions and Supply, 131
Desertion, 30, 40, 55, 76, 87
Diamond, "Duffy," 90
Dorchester, Lord, *see* Carleton, Sir Guy
Dryden, William A., 135, 180
Dufferin Street (Toronto), 15, 16, 80, 89
Dufferin, Manitoba, 65
Duncan, Lieutenant Francis, 40, 164
Durie, Lieutenant-Colonel William, 49, 50, 166, 169
Dymond, Roy James, 119
E.H.P., *see* Emergency Housing Project, 141-46

Index

Elgin, Lord (Governor General), 32–33
Elliot, Gilbert, 27–32, 76, 113, 159, 162, 177
Elliot, Gwen, 135
Emergency Housing Project (EHP), emergency housing, 141–47, 150, 154, 183
Enemy-Aliens, 13, 106–09, 111
    Registrar of "Enemy-Aliens," 107, 109
    Internment during First World War, 106–14, 175–77
    Internment at Stanley Barracks, 110-14, 176-77
Exhibition Camp, 88, 93–105, 113, 133
Exhibition Park, *see also* Canadian National Exhibition grounds, 11, 89, 90, 94
Exhibition Park Camp, *see* Exhibition Camp
Exhibition Place, *see also* Canadian National Exhibition grounds, 11, 14, 156
Exhibition Wharf, 81

Fargo, North Dakota, 65
Fenians, 37,
Fire, fires, firefighting duties, 10, 24, 32, 33, 87, 122, 136, 145, 156
    Fire at Stanley Barracks stables (1927), 118, 127
    Grandstand fire (1946), 139
Fitzgerald, Miss Jane, 32
Fives courts, 23, 24, 161
Fort Benton, Montana, 53
Fort Dufferin, Manitoba, 65
Fort Garry, *see* Stone Fort
Fort Henry (Kingston), 111
Fort Macleod, Alberta, 60
Fort Malden (Amherstburg), 149
Fort Rouillé, 15
Fort Toronto, *see* Fort Rouillé
Fort York, 9, 17, 18, 34, 37, 90, 115, 152, 178
Foster, Major T., 161
Foster, Mayor Thomas, 120
Found, Dr. Norman, 153, 184
Francis, Sergeant-Major Joe, 57
Fredericton, New Brunswick, 70–71
Freeling, Lieutenant Arthur H., 25, 27, 161

French, Lieutenant-Colonel/Commissioner George A., 49, 50, 53–56, 61
Fur trade, fur traders, 15

Garrison Common, the Common, 26, 28, 33–35, 42, 46–49, 67–69, 77, 79, 80, 88–90, 114, 115, 118, 122, 124, 135, 163, 177
Garrison Creek, 35
Garrison Reserve, *see* Reserve, military

Gathercole, Sergeant-Major Fred, 75
Gilman, Lieutenant-Colonel F., 118, 178
Glegg, Lieutenant Thomas, 21–23, 30, 160
Goodwin, Lieutenant-Colonel__, 45, 47, 49-51, 67, 165, 166
Governor General's Body Guard, 7, 34
Grand Trunk Railway, 56, 64
Guildwood Village, 14, 151, 153
Gzowski, Colonel Casimir S., 47–49, 79, 165

Hague Convention (1907), 108
    Rules concerning treatment of prisoners of war, 108
Halifax, Nova Scotia, 44, 45, 86, 111, 121, 122
Hamilton, Ontario, 18, 92
Hamilton, Colonel R.G., 45
Head, Sir Francis Bond, 18
Herbert, Major-General I.J.C., 82
Heritage Toronto, 155
His Majesty's Army and Navy Veterans' Society, 150, 184
Historic Fort York, *see also* Fort York, 13, 155
Hockey Hall of Fame, see National Hockey Hall of Fame horses, 20, 23, 26, 39, 48, 50, 61, 63–65, 86, 88, 90, 102, 115, 117, 118, 125, 127, 172
Horse shows, 115, 116, 118, 178
Horse Palace, 129
Hotel development plans for Stanley Barracks, 156
    HK Hotels of New York, 156
Housing (Toronto):
    Postwar housing shortage, 11, 139, 142, 145, 148

Emergency civilian housing, 11, 141–47, 154, 181, 183
Housing Authority (Toronto), 183
Hudson's Bay Company, 52
Hughes, Elwood, 129, 141, 180
Hughes, James L., 7
Hughes, Major-General Sam, 98
Huron, Lake, 15
Hussein, Youssef, 177

Industrial Exhibition Association, 67
Infantry School Corps: 7, 71, 78, 82, *see also* Royal Canadian Regiment
    "C" Company, 7, 78
Irwin, Major De la Cherois T., 49, 165

Jackson, Inspector Thomas R. (North-West Mounted Police), 57
Jameson Avenue (Toronto), 81
Johnson, Ed, 201
Jubilee Boulevard (Toronto), 121, 124

Kent, J.P., 141, 18
King Street (Toronto), 38, 78
Kingston, Ontario, 18, 50, 53–55, 57, 82, 86, 166
    School of Gunnery (Artillery school), 47, 49, 53, 57
Kingston Road (Toronto), 151, 153

Lake Shore Boulevard (Toronto), 11, 12, 142, 143
Langdon, James, 50
Laurier, Prime Minister Wilfrid, 87, 90, 173
Lessard, Lieutenant-Colonel F.L., 87, 88, 95, 172
Levis, Quebec, 92, 173
Limestone for building, 18
"Little Norway," 142, 144, 181
Locke, Harold V., 142, 144, 145, 147, 183
London, Ontario, 58, 59, 86, 171
London Exposition (1851), 36
Long Branch (Mimico), 141, 142, 144, 147
Lord Strathcona's Horse, 86
Lot Street (Toronto), 35
MacDonald, Eva, 184, 201

Macdonald, Prime Minister Sir John A., 10, 52–54, 166
Macdonald, Perly, 79, 81
Mackenzie, Dr. William Orde, 26, 27, 162
Manning Depot (C.N.E. Camp), 129, 130, 134
Marine Museum of Upper Canada, 13, 153–55
Massey, Governor General Vincent, 151
Massey-Harris Company, 148
Maxted, Mary, 178, 201
McCallum, Mayor Hiram, 146, 148, 182, 183
McFall, A.D., 152
Memorial Gates, *see* Stanley Barracks, gates
Middleton, Major-General Frederick D., 75
Miles, Captain Tom, 57
Military school (New Fort), 41, 48, 69, 70, 73
Military Service Act of 1917, 113
Militia Act of 1855, 41
Militia Act of 1883, 70
Militia Act of 1904, 92
Militia schools, *see* Military schools (New Fort)
Militia, Canadian, Active Militia, Permanent Active Militia 10, 34, 41, 48, 52, 57, 66, 72, 75, 77, 80, 82, 88, 126, 157, 166
Mimico, Ontario, 81, 141
Minister of Militia and Defence, 45, 51, 67, 70, 76, 80, 81, 90, 98, 164, 165, 169–71, 173
Minto, Fourth Earl of, 27
Minto, Second Earl of, 27
Miss War Worker Beauty Contest, 138
Montreal, Quebec, 27, 41, 45, 55, 61, 63, 70
Mountbatten, Earl of Burma, 154
Mounted Police, *see* North-West Mounted Police
Musical Ride, Dragoons' Musical Ride, 88, 115–18, 125, 156, 184
Musicians, *see* Band, regimental

N.W.M.P, *see* North-West Mounted Police
National Hockey Hall of Fame, 155
Natives, Native People, 15, 52, 53, 65

Index

New Fort, 9–14, 18–25, 27, 28, 30, 31, 34, 36–41, 45, 47–51, 57–67, 69–72, 74–79, 81–84, 87, 89, 92, 114, 119, 120, 143, 151, 153, 156, 161, 164, 170–71, see also Stanley Barracks
New Garrison Wharf, 25
Newark, Upper Canada, 16
Niagara Falls, 28
Niagara Falls, Ontario, 111
Niagara-on-the-Lake, Ontario, see Newark
Nicolls, Lieutenant-Colonel Gustavus, 18, 20, 160
North-West Mounted Police:
    Establishment, 10, 52, 53
    Pay, 54, 59
    Recruitment, recruits, 53, 55–58, 61–64
    Riding school at New Fort, 63–64
    Royal North-West Mounted Police (1904), 175
    Training at New Fort, 10, 58–65
    Uniforms, 53, 54, 57
North-West Rebellion (1885), 78
Northwest Territory, 10, 52–54, 166

Officers' quarters, see Stanley Barracks
OFPA, see Old Fort Protective Association
Old Fort, see also Fort York, 9, 15–18, 20–22, 24, 28, 34–37, 41, 45, 49, 89, 90, 114, 164, 166, 170, 173, 177
Old Fort Protective Association, 89, 90, 173
Ontario Motor League, 103
Ontario Rifle Association, 47, 48, 50, 67–69, 78, 170
Ontario, Lake, 9, 11, 15, 16, 28, 37–39
Ottawa, Ontario, 45, 48, 49, 51–55, 57, 67, 81, 82, 94, 107, 108, 110, 114, 115, 142, 158
Otter, Molly, 76, 86, 170, 172
Otter, Sir William Dillon: 41, 67–69, 71–76, 81, 84–90, 164, 169–73, 108–14, 176, 177
    Assigned to command "C" Company, 71
    At New Fort military school, 1860s, 73, 75
    Author of manual for Canadian militia, 72
    Commandant of Infantry School, 78, 84
    Director of internment operations, 108–14
    In South African War, 85, 86
    North-West Rebellion, 78
    Old Fort Protective Association, 89, 90
    Queen's Own Rifles Battalion, 41, 78
    Receives illuminated address from City of Toronto, 78
    Rifle range controversy, 78–81
    Secretary of Ontario Rifle Association, 67–69, 78

Palace of Industry, see Crystal Palace
Parker, Harry, 58
Parker, Constable William, 54, 58–64, 167–69
Parks Department, City of Toronto, 114
Parks Service, 149
Pellatt, Sir Henry M., 91, 177
Permanent Force (Canadian), 10, 12, 70, 71, 76–78, 82–92, 85, 91, 141, 158
Peter Street (Toronto), 35
Pier Museum, The (Toronto), 155
Police (Toronto), 32, 33, 45, 135, 146
Powell, Lieutenant-Colonel W., 66, 165, 169, 171
Princes' Gates (C.N.E.), 126, 130
Prisoners, 24, 33, 105, 108–13, 176
Provincial Agricultural Association: 35
    Annual fairs, 35, 67
    Establishment of (1846), 35, 36
Provincial Lunatic Asylum, 36

Quebec, Province of, 41, 43, 53, 71, 82, 86, 92, 176
Quebec City, 39, 166
Queen Street (Toronto), 16, 146
Queen's Own Rifles (2nd), see Regiments
Queen's Rangers, 16
Queenston limestone, 18

Range No. 1 Barracks, 19, 20, 22–24, 115, 156

Range No. 2 Barracks, 19, 24, 110, 115
RCAF, *see* Royal Canadian Air Force
RCAF Manning Depot, 129, 130, 134
RCD, *see* Royal Canadian Dragoons
RCR, *see* Royal Canadian Regiment
Rebellion Losses Bill (1849), 32
Rebellion, Lower Canada, *see* Rebellions of 1837–38
Rebellion, Upper Canada, *see* Rebellions of 1837–38
Rebellions of 1837–38, 9, 17, 25, 32
Red Cross, 130, 134
Red River Expedition (1870), 43, 46, 47, 53, 165
Regiments:
    2nd Battalion, Queen's Own Rifles, 7, 41, 78, 81, 91, 92, 173, 177
    6th Regiment, 54
    10th Light Dragoons, 57
    10th Royal Grenadiers, 7, 81, 171, 193
    13th Hussars, 37, 38, 57
    16th Imperials, 75
    16th Regiment, 37
    30th Regiment, 37, 37
    47th Regiment, 37
    48th Highlanders, Toronto Scottish Regiment, 7, 129, 177
    69th Regiment, 52
    83rd Regiment, 29
    93rd Highlanders, 24
    Regiment of Canadian Artillery (RCA), 71, 82, 174
    Royal Canadian Dragoons (RCD), 8, 10, 71, 82, 85–88, 90–92, 99, 105, 115–17, 125, 141
    Royal Canadian Regiment (RCR), 7, 8, 10, 71, 85, 87, 90–92, 99, 115, 170
    Royal Canadian Regiment of Infantry, 171
    Royal Canadian Rifles (60th), 37, 41
    Royal Grenadiers (10th), 7, 81
Reserve, Military, Garrison reserve, 16–18, 21, 24, 35, 36, 38, 43, 48, 65–68, 79, 89, 129, 141, 156, 163, 164, 169

Richmond, Duke of, 16, 159
Riel, Louis, 43
Rifle range, 8, 35, 49, 67, 69, 78–81, 94
Riley, R.E., 127, 128, 179
Robertson-Ross, Colonel Patrick, 52, 53, 165, 167
Royal Agricultural Winter Fair, 129, 134, 180
Royal Artillery, 38–41
Royal Canadian Air Force (RCAF), 129
Royal Canadian Artillery: 49, 53, 82, 99, 129
    "A" Battery, 49, 53
Royal Canadian Dragoons (RCD), *see* Regiments
Royal Canadian Engineers, 99, 126, 129
Royal Canadian Horse Artillery, 92
Royal Canadian Military Institute, 152
Royal Canadian Ordnance Corps, 129, 130
Royal Canadian Regiment (RCR), *see* Regiments
Royal Canadian Regiment of Infantry, 171
Royal Canadian Rifles (60th), 37, 41
Royal Corps of Engineers (British Army), 9, 18, 21, 23–25, 30, 36, 45
Royal Grenadiers (10th), 7, 81
Royal Irish Constabulary, 57, 166
Royal Military College, 171
Royal North-West Mounted Police (R.N.W.M.P.), 175
Royal Norwegian Air Force, 142
Royal visit (1901), 88
Royal visit (1939), 127
Royal Winter Fair, 115, 117, 125, *see also* Royal Agricultural Winter Fair
Russell, Lord John, 27
Russell, W. Howard, 37, 40, 164

Saint Jean, Quebec, 71
Saunders, Mayor Robert H., 141, 181, 182, 184
Scarborough, Ontario, 151, 153
Scoble, Colonel Thomas, 49–51, 62, 166, 169
Scoefield, Gunner __ ("A" Battery, RCA), 15
Second Canadian Contingent (First World War), 94

Index

Selby-Smyth, Major-General Edward, 66, 67, 69, 169, 170
"Sergeant Murphy" (horse), 115
Servants, 19, 31, 49, 73
Seven Years' War, 15
Shaw, Mayor John, 81, 171
Shevchenko, Taras, 114
Ship's Inn (Stanley Barracks), 155
Shuter, Lieutenant-Colonel E.H. "Ted," 126, 129 179–80
Simcoe, Lieutenant Governor John Graves, 15, 16, 35, 156, 157, 159
Skittle alley, skittles, 40, 164
Sleighing, 29, 118
Softball, 136
South African War, 86, 87, 172
Spark, Lieutenant-Colonel R., 24, 161
St. John's Garrison Church, 91
Stanley Barracks buildings:
    Barracks, 8, 18–20, 22–24, 28, 30, 31, 35, 37–40, 46–51, 61, 62, 66, 71, 74, 76, 87, 97, 109, 110, 114, 115, 118, 120, 122, 125–27, 143, 146, 149–51,156, 158, 160, 170, *see also* Range No. 1 and Range No. 2
    Canteen, 19, 71–73, 83
    Hospital, 18, 19, 40, 41, 50, 73, 110, 119, 125, 149
    Mess, 19, 24, 30, 31, 37, 47, 48, 64, 73, 74, 78, 83, 85, 125, 129,130, 137, 180
    Officers' quarters, 11, 19
    Stables, 20, 24, 39, 40, 41, 51, 94, 102, 118, 121, 122, 125–27, 136
Stanley Barracks:
    Construction of, 17–25, 160
    Demolition of, 11, 12, 141, 147–54, 183
    Fencing, 20
    Fortifications, 20, 37, 159, 160
    Gates (Memorial Gates), 20, 22, 50, 84, 96, 115, 118, 121, 122, 126, 127, 132, 151, 153, 184
    Parade square, 8, 9, 19, 21, 23, 127, 143, 149
    Water supply, 24, 25, 42, 71, 148
    Wells, 19, 24

Stanley, Frederick Arthur (Lord Stanley of Preston), 82, 171
Stanley Cup, 124, 171–72
Steele, Samuel B., 47, 54, 55, 57, 165, 168
Steer, Dorothy, *see* Brasier, Dorothy
Steer, Lieutenant-Colonel E. Arthur, 86, 90, 115, 172
Stevens, Daniel P., 86, 87, 172
Stone Fort (Fort Garry), 54, 55, 57, 65
Strachan Avenue (Toronto), 93
Strachan Avenue Cemetery (Military cemetery), 164, 190
Streetcar line controversy (1905), 89, 90

Tarte, Joseph-Israël, 87, 88
Tecumseh House (London, Ontario), 59
Timmis, Lieutenant-Colonel Reginald Symonds, 116–18, 127, 178
Toronto Board of Control, 148
Toronto City Council, *see* City Council, Toronto
Toronto Civic Historical Committee, 149, 152, 154, 155
Toronto Cricket Club, 69
Toronto Harbour, 9
Toronto Historical Board, 13, 155
Toronto Orchestral Association, 78
Toronto Receiving Station, 113
Toronto Volunteers, 47–48
Toronto Women's Patriotic League, 103
Treaty of Washington (1871), 44
Trent (British ship), 37
Turf Club, 48
Turofsky, Lou and Nat, 124

Ukrainian Canadian Civil Liberties Association, 114, 176
Ukrainian Canadian Foundation of Taras Shevchenko, 114

Valcartier, Quebec, 94, 98
Volunteers, Militia, 7, 48, 64, 78
Volunteers, Toronto, 35

Walsh, Major James (North-West Mounted Police), 55
War of 1812, 9, 17, 93, 153

Wartime Housing Ltd., 142, 183
Waterloo, Battle of, 165
Weir, John, 150
Weir, Mary, 150
Wellington, Duke of, 165
Wily, Lieutenant-Colonel Thomas, 45, 46, 49, 51
Winnipeg, Manitoba, 82, 86
Women's Canadian Historical Society, 153
Woodbine Racetrack, 89

Yonge Street (Toronto), 26, 155
York, Town of, 16, 17, 159
York Pioneer and Historical Society, 152
York, Battle of, 16
York, Duke of, 16
Yukon Field Force, 82, 86

Zootsuiters reported at Stanley Barracks, 146

ABOUT THE AUTHOR

ALDONA SENDZIKAS is the former assistant curator of Historic Fort York. She has also been the curator of the restored Second World War submarines USS *Pampanito* (SS-383) in San Francisco and USS *Bowfin* (SS-287) at Pearl Harbor. She is currently an associate professor in the Department of History at the University of Western Ontario, and is the author of *Lucky 73: USS* Pampanito's *Unlikely Rescue of Allied POWs in World War II* (University Press of Florida, 2010).

OF RELATED INTEREST

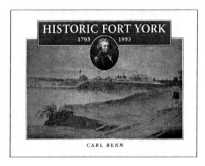

Historic Fort York, 1793–1993
Carl Benn
978-0-92047-479-2
$29.95

Fearing an American invasion of Upper Canada, John Graves Simcoe had Fort York built in 1793 as an emergency defensive measure. That act became the first step in the founding of modern Toronto. In this book, Carl Benn explores the dramatic roles Fort York played in the frontier war of the 1790s, the birth of Toronto, the War of 1812, the Rebellion of 1837, and the defence of Canada during the American Civil War, and describes how Toronto's most important heritage site came to be preserved as a tangible link to Canada's turbulent military past.

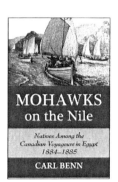

Mohawks on the Nile
Natives Among the Canadian Voyageurs in Egypt, 1884–1885
Carl Benn
978-1-55002-867-6
$40.00

Mohawks on the Nile explores the absorbing history of sixty aboriginal men who left their occupations in the Ottawa River timber industry to participate in a military expedition on the Nile River in 1884-1885. Their objective was to reach Khartoum, capital of the Egyptian province of Sudan. Their mission was to save its governor general, Major-General Charles Gordon, besieged by Muslim forces inspired by the call to liberate Sudan from foreign control by Muhammad Ahmad, better known to his followers as the "the Mahdi."

Toronto
The Way We Were
Mike Filey
978-1-55002-842-3
$45.00

In one lavishly illustrated volume, Toronto historian Mike Filey serves up the best of his meditations on everything from the Royal York Hotel, the Flatiron Building, and the Necropolis to Massey Hall, the Palais Royale, and the Canadian National Exhibition, with streetcar jaunts through Cabbagetown, the Annex, Rosedale, and Little Italy and trips down memory lane with Mary Pickford, Glenn Miller, Bob Hope, and Ed Mirvish.

Available at your favourite bookseller.

What did you think of this book? Visit www.dundurn.com for reviews, videos, updates, and more!